CONTENTS

PART FIVE: KEEPING IT ALL STRAIGHT

HELP! I NEED TO...	TURN TO PAGE...
Plan a Rite of Acceptance	47 and 167
Plan a Rite of Sending for Election	55 and 172
Plan a Scrutiny rite	30 and 175
Lead a dismissal session	178
Lead a catechetical session	179
Know how to know if they're ready	113
Find sponsors	91
Start a team Get the parish more involved	84
Learn what to do with the baptized folks	146
Know what to do with children	133
Learn how to start a year-round process	165
Figure out how to get started in the first place	97

For twenty years I have been searching for a resource that was concise, logical, and informative regarding the entire RCIA process. *The Way of Faith* is that resource!

■ DOUGLAS J. REATINI, Director, Office of Worship
Diocese of Saint Petersburg

The Way of Faith is a terrific book—insightful, practical, and focused on the things that matter. (It's funny, too.) The chapter on how to do parish liturgy well is alone worth the price, but the thoughtful and hands-on guidance for RCIA teams and parish leaders makes this truly extraordinary.

■ MSGR. VINCENT RUSH, Pastor, Our Lady of Grace Church
West Babylon, New York

Imagine a single sourcebook that combines good theory and tested pastoral strategies in an engaging and readable format! Now buy it! *The Way of Faith* is a "must have" for parishes that take Christian initiation seriously.

■ REV. ROBERT DUGGAN, Presbyter of the Archdiocese of Washington, DC

Here is the book I wish I could have read when I was first learning about the RCIA. Nick Wagner has written both an easy-to-navigate guide for those working with the catechumenate for the first time as well as an in-depth study for those well-versed in its principles and process.

■ KATHY HENDRICKS, author, speaker, catechetical leader

Like Nick Wagner, I have a "disreputable past" when it comes to implementing the RCIA back in the day. If I had had a copy of *The Way of Faith*, I could have avoided a lot of mistakes and had a lot of my own murky ideas about the RCIA clarified and corrected. This book provides newcomers to the RCIA ministry with the valuable guidance they will need to understand the Rite and to implement it most effectively.

■ JOE PAPROCKI, Associate Director of Catechetical Services, Loyola Press

I am very impressed with *The Way of Faith*. It is a wonderful book full of very practical information.

■ THOMAS RICHSTATTER, OFM, Professor of liturgy and sacramental theology

The Way of Faith is the best, most practical piece of writing I've ever seen on matters RCIA. This resource is just what the doctor ordered. Bravo!

■ BERNADETTE GASSLEIN, Editor of *Celebrate!*

This book could really be titled "The Catechumenate for Dummies!" It is a great resource that describes the process in detail, gives practical applications, and explores pastoral situations.

■ TISH SCARGILL, Director of Catechetical Ministries
Diocese of Monterey, California

*The book is dedicated
to Diana,
my companion,
coconspirator,
and inspiration.*

Cover image: ©iStockphoto.com/Jay Stevens

To access the online resources listed in this book, go to TeamRCIA.com and use this password: romans6311

Second printing 2008

Twenty-Third Publications
A Division of Bayard
One Montauk Avenue, Suite 200
New London, CT 06320
(860) 437-3012 or (800) 321-0411
www.23rdpublications.com

ISBN 978-1-58595-710-1
Library of Congress Catalog Card Number: 2008929289
Printed in the U.S.A.

PART ONE

INTRODUCTION

1 Moving from a Good RCIA to an Excellent Initiation Process

first "discovered" the catechumenate when I went to a diocesan workshop in the late 1970s. Of course, I didn't know it was called *catechumenate* back then. All I knew was there was a diocesan meeting on one of the changes initiated by Vatican II. And somewhere about halfway through the presentation, the priest who's leading us through the rite says something about the "cateh-somethings" (the folks who want to be Catholic) leaving church in the middle of Mass! Before the collection! Whoa!

If I were a cartoon character, you would have seen a big bright light bulb appear over my head at that moment. It dawned on me that dismissing the catechumens from Mass would be so *shocking* to Catholics that it had huge potential for igniting dozens and hundreds and maybe thousands of conversion experiences.

In most parishes, this practice is so common now that it has become unremarkable. But try to remember or imagine the church of the 1970s in middle America. It was a *very* structured, top-down, by-the-book kind of place, at least where I grew up. The reforms of the Second Vatican Council, however, soon began to have an impact in local parishes. Folks who were there have differing stories about how well or badly the changes were handled, but one thing everyone agrees on is there were a lot of changes. With any change there is struggle. Even those who were highly enthused about the vision of the Council would feel the strain of so much newness all at once. It was in *that* moment that the reform of the adult initiation process began to trickle down to ordinary parishes.

While I was excited about the possibilities this new rite could offer my parish and the parishes of my diocese, many parish leaders were plain worn out by the time the RCIA was handed down to us.

THE "GRAB THE LAST BOTTLE" APPROACH

Did you ever get invited to a party you didn't really want to go to? You knew you had to go, but you were praying for a small lightning storm to knock out the power around town on the day of. No such luck. Sunny beautiful day. Still, you procrastinated. The hour approached, and you'd find yourself completely immersed in cleaning the cabinet under the kitchen sink that you'd been meaning to get to for years. You looked at your watch and suddenly "remembered" you had to be somewhere. You dashed into the shower, threw on some clothes, and were almost out the door when you remembered you really should bring a gift. You really should. Your eye fell on the small wine rack atop the refrigerator. One bottle left that someone brought to *your* last party. You grabbed it, blew the dust off, and headed out the door.

That feels to me like the way a lot of parishes started their catechumenate processes. Reluctantly, last minute, not well thought out. Certainly we've come a long way, and fewer and fewer parishes today could be described as implementing the RCIA so haphazardly. There are even many parishes today that would say they are doing a good job with the catechumenate.

Good is not good enough

And that's a problem. We've moved from the "grab the last bottle" approach to doing some actual planning of the way the rites are celebrated and the catechumens are formed. This is such a step up from where we were that we've become satisfied. We've gone from nothing at all, to slap-dash, last minute, to not so bad. But is that enough? What would it take to have an excellent catechumenate? What would it take to have the best initiation process your parish is capable of?

It would take a lot. No kidding, it would take a lot of time and energy. And aren't we doing okay as it is? Some regions have tons of people joining the parish, and, amazingly, enough volunteers (barely) to help out so a few people aren't doing all the work by themselves.

You deserve a breather, you really do. Some folks have been working in initiation ministry almost non-stop for 20 or 30 years. For some of you reading this book, you might be the sole reason your parish has any catechumenate process at all. If you haven't been thanked enough for that ministry (and you should have been), THANK YOU! Because of your dedication, we are in a place where we are able to move on.

And move on we must. In his book, *Good to Great*, Jim Collins says, "Good is the enemy of great. And that is one of the key reasons why we have so little that becomes great" (p. 1). We will never have great catechumenate processes if we are satisfied with good-enough ones. And only an excellent catechumenate process will consistently and powerfully lead not just the catechumens but the entire parish to an experience of profound, intimate communion with Christ. When that light bulb clicked on in my head, that's what I saw—radical, passionate conversion to Christ on a massive scale. The RCIA envisions nothing less.

An excellent catechumenate does take work. But it doesn't take miracles. To get started, you need two things, two gifts, which the Holy Spirit will be happy to give to you if you ask. Maybe you already have them.

1. You need the gift of humility.
2. You need the gift of passion.

If you have these two gifts, or if you are willing to pray for them, you can learn everything else you need to know to make the catechumenate a great process of conversion in your community.

2 Guide to the Catechumenate

A friend of mine likes to hunt, but he's a city boy. Whenever he ventures out into the wilderness, he hires someone who knows the area. So on one trip, he and a group of buddies are being led through the woods by a local guide. After a while, my friend realizes the group is lost and confronts the guy.

"You told us you were the best guide in Colorado!" says my hunter friend.

"I am," replies the guide, "but I think we're in Wyoming now."

An important part of any journey is knowing where *not* to go. You don't want to wind up in Wyoming if your destination is Colorado.

ROMAN CATHOLIC INTELLIGENCE AGENCY— WHAT RCIA IS NOT

The catechumenate process is so often referred to as the "RCIA" that our understanding of what it is has become blurred. We don't always remember what the initials mean, and it is too easy to project on them whatever we want them to mean.

So here is a quick list of what the RCIA is not.

- It is not an adult confirmation program
- It is not an adult education program
- It is not a marriage preparation program, even if one person in the couple is not Catholic

- It is not CCD for adult Catholics who "dropped out" after confirmation
- It is not a place for sponsors or spouses to "catch up" on facts of the faith
- It is not a small faith sharing community
- It is not a support group for dealing with emotional distress
- It is not a class
- It is not a club
- It is not a program for making Protestants into Catholics

Welcome to the church's transmogrifier

So what is the RCIA? If you are a *Calvin and Hobbes* fan, you'll understand when I tell you that the RCIA is a transmogrifier (see tinyurl.com/2cxafa). A transmogrifier is an upside-down cardboard box with a dial drawn onto the side. According to Calvin, "You step into the chamber, set the appropriate dials, and it turns you into whatever you'd like to be" (*Calvin and Hobbes*, March 23, 1987). In a similar way, the RCIA transmogrifies an unbeliever into a believer, a person of little or no faith into a disciple of Jesus Christ.

Conversion machine

Go get your copy of the rite and look at paragraph 1. It says so right there:

> The rite of Christian initiation…is designed for adults who…consciously and freely seek…[to] enter the way of faith and conversion.

Whenever we refer to a line from a ritual text, we always refer to the paragraph number, not the page number. Several publishers have published the RCIA, and the page numbering is different in each edition. The paragraph numbers are consistent.

The RCIA is a transmogrification machine. Or if you prefer, a conversion process. You put the "Calvins" into it, and disciples come out of it.

Of course, the process is not a cardboard box. It's much more complex than that, and oftentimes we don't get disciples in the end. But that is what the process is built to do—make disciples. Unlike Calvin's box, you cannot just turn the dial and get whatever you want at the end. The process only has one setting: Disciples. If we put folks who are already disciples into the process, it won't make them "better" disciples. That's not what the process is designed to do.

Or, to return to our hunter story, if we want to hunt in Colorado, we have to be sure our guide knows how to move around Colorado. We have to be passionate about using the RCIA as a conversion process and only as a conversion process.

I think that word "conversion" is where we sometimes go astray and wind up in Wyoming. Because aren't we all in need of conversion? Isn't discipleship a lifelong conversion journey? Well, yes and no.

Grab your copy of the rite again, and flip to the back. In the appendix titled "National Statutes for the Catechumenate," paragraph 2, read the following:

> The term "convert" should be reserved strictly for those converted from unbelief to Christian belief....

There is an initial conversion, after which you can never be "converted" again. You can be a bad convert, and your conversion may require some serious maintenance. You can fall away and even deny your conversion ever happened. And these are serious issues that need to be remedied. But the catechumenate is not the remedy. The catechumenate is a process of conversion for those who have never believed—even a little.

So in the church's transmogrification process, we put catechumens in the transmogrifier, adjust the dials, and take out disciples. And what exactly goes on inside that amazing "cardboard box"?

That's what we're going to explore.

PART TWO

THE STAGES OF THE CATECHUMENATE

3 Changing the Light Bulbs: A Catholic's Guide to Conversion

You've heard this one, haven't you? How many Catholics does it take to change a light bulb?

CHANGE??!!?

If you grew up like I did, a Catholic school boy in the middle of the Midwestern United States, your life had a single purpose—to get to heaven. You got to heaven by believing in and living the eternal, unchanging doctrines of the church. "Change" was not part of the program.

But a simple look at the Gospel shows us all of Christian life is fundamentally about change. We are baptized into the death and resurrection of Jesus Christ. Change doesn't get any more radical than that.

As we mentioned in the previous chapter, there is only one conversion. But after the initial conversion, there are degrees of change or ongoing conversion. There are the steps of conversion that lead up to a profound and intimate communion with Jesus Christ. Following that, there are steps that are not so much about conversion, per se, as much as a deepening and remembering of our initial conversion to Christ.

The first part, the initial process of conversion to Christ, is what the catechumenate is all about. Now, if you and I were in the same room right now, you'd see my arms waving and hear my voice rising. *Conversion* is what we are all about as Christians. Conversion to Christ is totally, totally *awesome*. That's a word we have to recover from pop culture. It should be reserved only for this tremendous, life-changing, earth-shattering process. It is the word used by

Cyril, Ambrose, Chrysostom, and Theodore, among others—the Fathers of the fourth century who preached great mystagogical homilies (homilies that help us remember the mystery and awesomeness of our conversion).

Conversion to Christ is an awesome change. It is the most awesome change we will ever experience. This change doesn't just happen, though. It is, for most people, a gradual process that occurs over several stages. Let's look at each one.

OUTLINE FOR CHRISTIAN INITIATION OF ADULTS

» Period of Evangelization and Precatechumenate

This is a time, of no fixed duration or structure, for inquiry and introduction to Gospel values, an opportunity for the beginnings of faith.

FIRST STEP: acceptance into the order of catechumens

This is the liturgical rite, usually celebrated on some annual date or dates, marking the beginning of the catechumenate proper, as the candidates express and the Church accepts their intention to respond to God's call to follow the way of Christ.

» Period of the Catechumenate

This is the time, in duration corresponding to the progress of the individual, for the nurturing and growth of the catechumens' faith and conversion to God; celebrations of the word and prayers of exorcism and blessing are meant to assist the process.

SECOND STEP: election or enrollment of names

This is the liturgical rite, usually celebrated on the First Sunday of Lent, by which the Church formally ratifies the catechumens' readiness for the sacraments of initiation and the catechumens, now the elect, express the will to receive these sacraments.

» Period of Purification and Enlightenment

This is the time immediately preceding the elects' initiation, usually the Lenten season preceding the celebration of this initiation at the Easter Vigil; it is a time of reflection, intensely centered on conversion, marked by celebration of the scrutinies and presentations and of the preparation rites on Holy Saturday.

THIRD STEP: celebration of the sacraments of initiation

This is the liturgical rite, usually integrated into the Easter Vigil, by which the elect are initiated through baptism, confirmation, and the Eucharist.

» Period of Postbaptismal Catechesis or Mystagogy

This is the time, usually the Easter season, following the celebration of initiation, during which the newly initiated experience being fully a part of the Christian community by means of pertinent catechesis and particularly by participation with all the faithful in the Sunday eucharistic celebration.

— *Rite of Christian Initiation of Adults*

4 Stage One: Find a Light that Needs Changing

As Christians, we live in the light. Have you ever heard that before? Do you believe it? What does it really mean?

Well, it's a metaphor, right? It can mean a few different things because that's how metaphors work. For me, it mostly means I have hope. I have bad days, dark days, days when I stub my toe looking for the light switch. But I always know there is a switch. And I always know the light will go on when I find it. So, I'm a pretty good Christian who spends a lot of time cursing the darkness. But it's not really darkness, is it? Not if I know how to turn on the light.

Because we live in the light, because we have this constant hope, I think we tend to forget that there are loads of people who live in the dark. Real dark. They don't know there is a switch. They don't know that light is possible. If we mostly hang out with other Christians or other people of hope, we can tend to pass right by these souls-in-darkness without even realizing it. Or if we do see them, we think we can just show them the switch and they'll be able to turn on the light themselves. Sometimes we call that ministry.

BECOMING BEARERS OF GOOD NEWS

Of course, it is not helpful to tell those who live in darkness to pray more or to go to church more or to stop sinning or to read the Bible. Those are all switches that work for us. They won't work for them, because they don't know there is light. They don't know there is hope. They don't know there is Jesus.

The very first thing we have to do is bring hope or good news. How do we do that? That's the $64 million question. The answer is, it depends. It depends on the soul-in-darkness in front of you and what his or her needs are. Does he need food? Does she need child care? Does he need a job? Does she need counseling for depression? Does he need someone to accept him as he is? Does she need to be loved? The darkness people live in is specific to each person. There isn't a standard, one-size-fits-all darkness. And so there isn't a standard, one-size-fits all conversion process.

Each conversion process begins with us listening to those who are in pain. We strain to hear exactly where the pain is. And, as best we are able, we try to empathize with the pain.

Really, the precatechumenate or inquiry stage has no other agenda than that. You can buy books and go to workshops on what to do during the precatechumenate, and I'll even try to give you some ideas here. But the RCIA itself says: "This is a time, of no fixed duration or structure, for inquiry…" (RCIA, 7).

This is *their* inquiry, not ours. The souls-in-darkness get to ask us questions. We don't ask them too many questions. That comes later.

LIVING LIKE A TURNIP HEAD

Ready for another metaphor? Let's say you are sitting around minding your own business, on a park bench maybe. This bus pulls up to the entrance of the park. It is a tour bus for a group of turnip fanatics who are in town for a convention. They get off the bus wearing turnip t-shirts, turnip-shaped hats, and turnip-colored backpacks. They start playing catch with turnips. There are these wacko turnip people everywhere. Finally your curiosity gets the better of you, and you ask one of the guys waiting his turn for turnip volleyball, "Hey, what's with all the turnips?" And he tells you how a friend of his introduced him to a turnip diet. He lost 300 pounds, met his wife at a turnip recipe exchange group, kicked his drug habit with the help of his turnip gardening club, and, most of all, realized that becoming a "turnip head" meant he'd never be alone again for the rest of his life.

So you think the guy has bigger problems than weight gain and drugs, and you back off kind of quickly. But then later in the week you run across another turnip head. And some guy at work shows up with a turnip pin on his lapel. You find out your son is hanging out with turnip heads at school. And all these people seem completely happy and at peace.

So you walk up to the guy at work one day and ask, "Really, what is it with all you turnip people?"

Pope Paul VI wrote a letter in 1978 in which he was more or less asking Christians if we are as visible in the world as the metaphorical turnip heads and what would happen if we were. He said:

> Take a Christian or a handful of Christians who, in the midst of their own community, show their capacity for understanding and acceptance, their sharing of life and destiny with other people, their solidarity with the efforts of all for whatever is noble and good.
>
> Let us suppose that, in addition, they radiate in an altogether simple and unaffected way their faith in values that go beyond current values, and their hope in something that is not seen and that one would not dare to imagine.
>
> Through this wordless witness these Christians stir up *irresistible questions* in the hearts of those who see how they live:
>
> - Why are they like this?
> - Why do they live in this way?
> - What or who is it that inspires them?
> - Why are they in our midst?
>
> Such a witness is already a silent proclamation of the Good News and a very powerful and effective one.
>
> Here we have an initial act of evangelization.
>
> The above questions will ask,
>
> - whether they are people to whom Christ has never been proclaimed,
> - or baptized people who do not practice,
> - or people who live as nominal Christians but according to principles that are in no way Christian,
> - or people who are seeking, and *not without suffering,* something or someone whom they sense but cannot name.
>
> Other questions will arise, deeper and more demanding ones, questions evoked by this witness which involves presence, sharing, solidarity, and which is an essential element, and generally the first one, in evangelization.
>
> (*On Evangelization in the Modern World,* 21; emphasis added)

EVANGELIZATION

There is a really interesting passage in the RCIA. If you flip open to paragraph 36 and skip down to the second sentence, you'll see what I mean.

> [The inquiry period] is a time of evangelization....

If we take Pope Paul VI's letter seriously, all of Christian life is a time of evangelization. That means we are always in the "Period of Evangelization and Precatechumenate." Keep reading, and look at our job description during this "period."

> [F]aithfully and constantly the living God is proclaimed [by us; all the time] and Jesus who he has sent for the salvation of all [is also proclaimed; by us; all the time].

So then what happens just by us living as Christians (as the turnip heads live like turnip heads), "those who are not yet Christians [have] their hearts opened by the Holy Spirit" (RCIA, 36).

I think that's interesting because it makes every Christian a minister of the inquiry period. Just as the turnip heads are always acting like turnip heads and attracting new people to their way of life, all of us are always acting like Christians, attracting new people to Christ. We don't attract people to Christ by holding precatechumenate classes. We don't have a defined inquiry "period." The inquiry period is an ongoing cycle that never ends. It is the way of Christian living.

Many times inquirers come to us at, what is for them, the very end part of the inquiry period. They have been evangelized by someone else and have had many of their fundamental questions answered. The questions they have for us, the "official" initiation ministers, are more about procedure and next steps.

There are those who really have those initial questions Pope Paul VI listed, who are searching for an answer, and for whom we may be the first evangelists.

We also get a number of tourists, people who are curious about Catholics, but, at least right now, have no desire to live the life. We get all of these various types of inquirers, and you can probably think of a few more. So how do you know who to accept into the catechumenate? It all depends on what happens during the inquiry period.

THE INQUIRY "SESSION"

This next section is a struggle for me to write. I don't really think there is a good way to give a step-by-step outline of what happens during the inquiry period. As soon as I write down steps, I realize I probably won't follow them the next time I'm confronted with a real inquirer. It's kind of like trying to describe dating. 1. Call the datee. 2. Suggest pizza and a movie. 3. Shower and shave. 4. Arrive at datee's place on time. 5. Exit car....

And I've never been on the same date twice. I'd have to write an entirely different list of steps for the second date. You get the idea.

So here are some general guidelines. Read them, and then promise me you will adapt them to fit the inquirers who actually show up in your life.

Call the datee

You need to pursue the inquirer in much the same way a suitor would pursue a date. You want to initiate contact enough so the other person knows you are interested, but you don't want to seem like a stalker. Some parishes have weekly meetings for the inquirers. For some inquirers, that's way too much commitment. Discern with each person to see what might feel right.

Suggest pizza and a movie

The operative word here is "suggest." The inquirers want to know something about Catholics. However, they may not be sure exactly what. You can offer some suggestions. But first, you have to get to know them a little. Perhaps they want to know about the Bible. Or Mass. Or Jesus. Or the pope. Ask a little, listen more.

Shower and shave

Can I share a secret? Promise not to tell anyone. I have some *issues* with the Roman Catholic Church. Don't get me wrong. I love being Catholic, but there are one or two things I'd do differently if they ever asked me. But the inquiry period is *not* the time to air all our dissatisfactions. We want to put our best foot forward with the inquirers. So what's best about us?

PRAYER

One of the things we do really well as Catholics is pray. Our inquiry sessions should include prayer, and the prayer forms and styles should change as the relationship with the inquirers changes. Our prayer might grow from a simple, single intercession to evening prayer based on the Liturgy of the Hours.

SCRIPTURE

Another thing we do really well as Catholics is tell stories. First, listen to the inquirers' stories. Then tell one of your own. Then tell one of the church's—from Scripture or from the lives of the saints. You don't necessarily need a Bible for this, but as the relationship grows, I think you would use a Bible more and more often.

SERVICE

As we tell more of our stories and the stories of the church, it will become evident to the inquirers that Catholics serve others, especially the poor. Part of their inquiry period might include joining some parishioners in their regular service activities. Or a "session" might be coffee with one of the social justice activists in your parish. Or a "session" might be accompanying the ministers who take Communion to the homebound.

COMMUNITY

We Catholics have a lot of relationships. Make sure the inquirers experience some of that. Inquiry can start out as a series of one-on-one "dates," but it should eventually evolve to include others in the community. The inquirers don't always have to go out with you. Ask some parishioners to invite the inquirers over for dinner or to a parish social event. If you sense an inquirer is getting ready to move to the next stage—the catechumenate—you will want to start including potential sponsors in your sessions.

Arrive at datee's place on time

We must always keep in mind this period is about *them*. We go to their front door. That is, we listen to their questions and concerns. If we don't know the answer, we find out in a timely fashion and get them the answer as soon as we can. We don't make them come to us, and we don't try to force them to have the questions we want them to have. Every session should include a time for them to ask questions and a time for us to follow up with answers from previous sessions.

Exit the car

And exit the parish. The inquiry session can happen anywhere. There's no rule that it has to be on parish property. Meet at a bar or a coffee shop. Meet at a parishioner's home. You could even meet for movie and pizza for real. Of course, there is nothing to stop you from choosing a movie that is likely to raise faith issues that would get discussed over the pizza. Be creative. Surprise your "date."

CRITERIA FOR READINESS

At some point the inquirers will have their questions answered, and they will be ready to move to another stage. For some, that stage is somewhere else in their lives, apart from us. For others, they will be ready to become catechumens.

I once asked a catechumenate team how they determined if an inquirer was ready to become a catechumen. Their answer, more or less, was that the inquirers attended the requisite number of precatechumenate classes. I tried to get them to expand their understanding of readiness, and I suggested they might want to develop a set of criteria for deciding who would celebrate the Rite of Acceptance and who would remain in the precatechumenate. One very nice man turned blue with shock. He could hardly speak. "You don't mean that *I* am supposed to decide who becomes a catechumen, do you?"

Indeed, I meant exactly that. Not all by himself, of course, but certainly him. And you. And anyone who is called to this ministry. That's *why* the Holy Spirit called us. We don't get to accept the role and shirk the responsibility.

However, it's not like picking the right number on the roulette wheel. There are actually guidelines to help us discern who is ready for the catechumenate.

Ritual questions

The door to each next stage of the process is a rite. In each rite, there are entry questions. To go through the door, the candidate needs to answer the questions. So the first step to determining readiness for the catechumenate is to ask the entry questions from the Rite of Acceptance into the Order of Catechumens. Of course, be a little creative with this. Don't haul out your ritual book and start "teaching the test." Read over the questions yourself, and try to understand what's being asked. Then look for lifestyle changes in the inquirers that "answer" the questions.

We'll look more closely at how to celebrate the rites in Part 3. But for now, for your discernment criteria, turn to the "Opening Dialogue" of the Rite of Acceptance (50). The presider asks the candidate what he wants from God's church. "Faith" is given as the sample answer, but the candidate might have something else he is looking for. The sections in small print give some other sample answers. The point is, throughout their inquiry, you should be paying attention to everything the inquirers say and do that might indicate what it is they really want.

The next question is what "faith" (could be something else) offers you. Also pay attention to the way they live this answer. Does it ring true? Does it seem right? Does it seem genuine?

Watch. Listen closely. When you are pretty sure you know what an inquirer wants and how whatever he wants will (or won't) fill his desire, you'll have an idea about his readiness for the catechumenate.

Pastoral introduction

The second place to look for discernment criteria is the pastoral introduction to each rite. You can find these in the pages preceding each rite. The introduction to the Rite of Acceptance couldn't be any clearer:

> The prerequisite for making this first step is
> > that the beginnings of the spiritual life
> > and the fundamentals of Christian teaching
> > > have taken root in the candidates.
> Thus there must be evidence of the first faith...
> > and of an initial conversion
> > and intention to change their lives
> > and to enter into a relationship with God in Christ.
> Consequently, there must also be
> > evidence of the first stirring of repentance,
> > a start to the practice of calling upon God in prayer,
> > a sense of the Church,
> > and some experience of the company and spirit of Christians.... (42)

You can spend the inquiry time watching for all of these behaviors in the candidates. Those who are serious about the Christian life will be easy to spot. Those who need more time for the spiritual life to take root will also be easy to spot. Don't rush the process. If they aren't ready, it is a huge disservice to the inquirers to enroll them in the catechumenate.

Don't get confused about the "candidates." The RCIA uses the word "candidate" to refer to both unbaptized and baptized people.

A candidate is any person, baptized or unbaptized, who is the focus of one of the rites, such as the Rite of Acceptance or the Rite of Election.

We often use the word "candidate" to refer to someone who is completing their initiation or who is being received into the Catholic Church. That's fine. Just don't get confused when a rite meant for unbaptized people also refers to candidates for that rite.

It is a disservice because the catechumenate stage calls for a huge commitment, as we will see in the next section. We are asking the inquirers to die to
many (or even all) of the things they once held dear. That is very hard to do,
and it is only possible if they have the first stirrings of real faith. If we rush the
process, they will likely become discouraged and fall away or simply go through
the motions just to please us and get through it. Take your time.

Once the inquirers are ready, we celebrate the Rite of Acceptance with
them. We'll say more about the actual ritual later. For now, it's important to
know that the ritual marks their entrance into the next stage of the process—
the catechumenate.

5 Stage Two: Learning How to Change a Light Bulb

So now you've discerned who really wants to change their lifestyle, and you've celebrated the Rite of Acceptance with them. Now what? Once someone has the desire to change, whether they want to be a turnip head or a Christian, they need to learn how to change. The inquiry stage is all about someone deciding if he or she wants to live a different life. The catechumenate stage is lifestyle modification. You can think of the catechumenate stage like a training camp—because that's exactly what the RCIA calls it:

> The catechumenate is an extended period…aimed at training [the catechumens] in the Christian life. (75)

For some of us, especially those of us who have been Christians all our lives, and *especially* for those of us who were good in school, we tend to misread that paragraph. (In our heads, we unconsciously read different meanings, much like those pictures that, if you stare at them long enough, the image changes.) Based on the way a lot of catechumenate programs are run, this is what I think many of us see:

> The catechumenate is a *nine-month* period…aimed at *teaching* [the catechumens] *Catholic doctrine.* (75)

Teaching Catholic doctrine is certainly important, and it should be a solid part of the catechumenate. But it is not the whole of the catechumenate or even the bulk of it. The catechumenate is mostly about training in the Christian life.

The same paragraph goes on to list four elements that are essential to the Christian lifestyle training of the catechumen.

CATECHESIS

The first essential element in training for the Christian lifestyle is catechesis. Catechesis is hard to define. It is *not* religious education, but it includes religious education. Catechesis is more like teaching the way Jesus did. You hang out with fishermen, you learn how to fish. You hang out with baseball players, you learn how to play ball. You hang out with turnip heads, you become a turnip head. You hang out with healing preachers who spend their lives walking to Jerusalem, you tend to heal, preach, and head to where the cross is. Now don't misunderstand me. I'm not saying catechesis is *informal.* It is very formal. But its form is not a textbook or the catechism. Its form is the liturgical year. We go to the cross in a very disciplined and patterned way throughout the liturgical year. Within that form, catechumens are led

to an appropriate acquaintance
   with dogmas and precepts
but also a profound sense
   of the mystery of salvation…. (75.1)

The way they do this is by listening to, reflecting on, and seeing their lives through the lens of the word of God, especially the word as we hear it proclaimed throughout the Sundays of the liturgical year.

LIFESTYLE CHECK

So how do you know the catechumens are getting the dogmas and precepts? Well, how do you know fisher-trainees are getting the basics of fishing? They catch fish. Just so with catechumens, they act like basic Christians. The RCIA lists what it is people in the Christian community do:

- Pray
- Bear witness
- Set hopes on Christ
- See miracles
- Love their neighbors
- Suppress their egos (See 75.2)

And you can think of more. When the turnip head trainees start acting like turnip heads, people notice. Is anyone noticing the catechumens are acting like Christians? The bottom line is, are their new practices separating them from their old lives and integrating them into a new life—a new life within the Christian community?

PARTY!

Or maybe "celebrate!" is more appropriate. Either way, the new lifestyles the catechumens are experiencing should be making them joyful. And joyful people want to celebrate.

Joyfulness doesn't always come free of sadness or regret. A new turnip head might be sad at leaving his non-turnip days behind. Maybe he even has to leave some family or friends behind who don't understand this weird turnip thing he's into. But the overriding factor is the deep joy and peace he feels at his core.

Of course, that is exactly what Jesus promises us. An everlasting joy and a peace that surpasses all understanding. The rest of the world may not understand, but the Christian community does.

The most important thing we do as Christians is come together in worship to give joyful thanks to God for rescuing us. It is in worship where we learn the basic pattern of our Christian lifestyle. Trainees learn it in the manner of a beginning piano student or a new baseball player. More practiced Christians relearn a forgotten way of doing things and strengthen patterns they already know. The liturgy forms us in the right way to live.

The church has lots of celebrations that are "suitable" for the catechumens and strengthen them in their new lifestyle. We would expect to see joyful catechumens at services of the Word and in the Sunday assembly, participating in the worship of the all-loving Creator (see 75.3).

CHANGING LIGHT BULBS

In the same way a fisher is catching fish before getting the Association of Avid Anglers official certification, or turnip heads plant turnips before harvesting bushels of vegetables, catechumens are changing light bulbs—and the world—before baptism. Part of their training in the Christian lifestyle is to do things Christians do in the world: spread the Gospel, build up the church, and profess faith. They are doing all that stuff Paul VI talked about that stirs up the same *irresistible questions* that got the catechumens started on this path in the first place (see 75.4).

CRIB NOTES

Now take out your copy of the RCIA and read paragraph 75. Underline things. Make notes in the margin. Once you have, you can write a shorthand version of it on an index card or the palm of your hand. For the catechumens to be trained in the Christian life, we need to immerse them in four things:

1. Word

2. Community

3. Worship

4. Service

Can you see how this is going to take a lot longer than nine months? Can you see why this can't be taught from a book? How did we learn to pray? Or to build up our parishes? Or serve the needy in the world? And how long did it take us to learn? Even learning the "Word"—which you'd think might be text-based— can't really be taught from a book. Every day we learn what God's Word is for us. Every moment God is speaking a new, creative Word—a word that almost has no words.

CRITERIA FOR READINESS

The church says that those who are starting with no understanding at all of who God is have to enter into the full, formal process of the church that explains who Jesus is. That full, formal process is one complete cycle of a liturgical year in which the full mystery of Christ is revealed. And even that might not be enough. But it is the very least that is required.

Once you discern the catechumens are ready for the next stage of their journey, you would schedule them for the upcoming Rite of Election. We'll discuss the specifics of the rite later. For now, keep in mind that once the bishop declares the catechumens to be elect, they move into a final, forty-day period of intense preparation for initiation. Remember this period almost always takes place during the forty days of Lent.

Ritual questions

The Rite of Election is another doorway with another set of entry questions.

We'll look at the details of the Rite of Election and the Rite of Sending for Election in part 3. What concerns us now is the criteria for readiness the Rite of Election expects. Take a look at the ritual questions and ask yourself the deeper question behind the text. How do the lives of the catechumens answer the questions?

Open your RCIA, and turn to paragraph 131. Section B provides the questions for deliberation that the bishop might ask. There are three questions, and they reflect the four cornerstones of catechesis that we discussed earlier and that are outlined in detail in paragraph 75: word, service, community, and worship.

As the catechumens mature, you will want to be observing them carefully. You are looking at their behaviors as much as you are listening to what they are saying. If their actions are matching their words—if they are living out the word of God, the mission of Christ, the fellowship of the community, the action of worship—they are probably candidates for the Rite of Election.

> The period of catechumenate, beginning at acceptance into the order of catechumens and including both the catechumenate proper and the period of purification and enlightenment after election or enrollment of names, should extend for at least one year of formation, instruction, and probation. Ordinarily this period should go from at least the Easter season of one year until the next; preferably it should begin before Lent in one year and extend until Easter of the following year.
>
> *National Statutes for the Catechumenate, 6*

Pastoral introduction

As with the previous stage, the next stage lays out criteria in the pastoral introduction. Turn to paragraph 120. Here again, the elements of paragraph 75 are reiterated:

Before the rite of election is celebrated,
the catechumens are expected to have undergone
　a conversion in mind
　and in action
and to have developed
　a sufficient acquaintance with Christian teaching
　as well as a spirit of faith and charity.

You can use this as a checklist to discern readiness. However, be careful that you keep the "acquaintance with Christian teaching" in balance with the other aspects of their formation. If they know all the doctrines but haven't had a true conversion of thought and action, they are not yet ready.

Once the catechumens are ready, it is time to schedule them for the Rite of Election. Once they are elect, they have moved into the next stage of their formation, the period of purification and enlightenment.

6

Stage Three: Basking in the Light

O kay, you've spent all this time training the catechumens to be experts in light bulb-changing procedures (evangelization and conversion). You are pretty confident they are able to go out into the world to be change agents.

There are a few important things that you as a parish leader need to stay focused on in this stage. First, this is not a time for catching up on catechesis the elect may have missed during the previous stage. If they aren't fully catechized, they are not valid candidates for the rite of election.

Also, entering this stage is a *big deal.* (I know, it's all a big deal, but this is a really big deal.) There is no turning back after the Rite of Election. When the catechumens sign their names in the Book of the Elect, they are making a formal, lifetime commitment.

Finally, this is a period of spiritual preparation. The RCIA doesn't exactly say *how* to do the spiritual preparation, so we have to be a little creative. That's good news and bad news. Room for creativity means you can adapt the spiritual preparation of your candidates to fit their specific needs. The bad news is without a given structure, we can easily get off track.

So to keep us on track, let's first recall *what* we are preparing the (unbaptized) candidates for. We are preparing the catechumens to live like Jesus. We are preparing them for initiation into the mission Jesus inaugurated. And that mission is primarily to announce the good news to those who have not yet heard it.

In the Acts of the Apostles, the last thing Jesus says to the disciples is, "You will receive power when the Holy Spirit comes upon you, and you will be my witnesses…to the ends of the earth" (1:8).

Job One: Be witnesses. In the way we live, the way we talk, the way we act, in all we do. That's the life we are preparing the catechumens for.

If the goal, then, is evangelization, what elements are necessary for their preparation? You need the 3Rs:

Rites

Reflection (mystagogical)

Retreats

RITES

The most significant aspect of the formation of the elect is the rituals they will celebrate. (We'll cover these in depth in part three.) There are four major rites (required) and several minor rites (optional).

Major rites

RITE OF ELECTION

The first rite for those entering this stage is, of course, the Rite of Election (RCIA, 118-137). This usually takes place on the First Sunday of Lent, usually at the diocesan cathedral. It is called "election" because the church chooses from among the catechumens those who will be baptized at the next Easter Vigil. The church makes this choice based on the choice God has made. The church is acting in the name of God, and therefore a prayerful discernment of those to be enrolled is essential.

The church (that's us) is going to make its choice based on three factors:

- the testimony of the godparents
- the prayerful judgment of the rest of the team and the parish community
- the catechumens' reaffirmation of their intention

It is difficult to overstate the importance and solemnity of this discernment. When Jesus left us with the mandate to "go and baptize," it was not meant to be an indiscriminate sprinkling of anyone who wanted to become Catholic. To baptize means to *plunge* into the paschal mystery—the death and resurrection of Jesus. It is not a small thing. For the early Christians, baptizing someone could be actually sending that person to his or her death. At the very least, we are immersing them in a life of self-sacrifice, never again to be lived solely for their own sakes. The stakes are high.

Because the stakes are high, the rite says:

> Before the rite of election the bishop, priests, deacons, catechists, godparents, and the entire community, in accord with their respective responsibilities and in their own way, should, after considering the matter carefully, arrive at a judgment about the catechumens' state of formation and progress. After the election, they should surround the elect with prayer, so that the entire Church will accompany and lead them to encounter Christ. (121)

Note that the rite includes the bishop in this discernment process. In the rite, the bishop will formally declare the church's approval of the catechumens. Therefore, the discernment is to be genuine.

> Therefore to exclude any semblance of mere formality from the rite, there should be a deliberation prior to its celebration to decide on the catechumens' suitableness. (122)

Godparents

Pay some attention to paragraph 123. The text says that before the Rite of Election, the catechumens choose their godparents. This is confusing for some teams because they assume the sponsors will be the godparents. They may well be, but that decision is up to the catechumens.

INVOLVING THE BISHOP IN DISCERNMENT

At first, it may seem difficult to involve the bishop in the discernment of the readiness of the catechumens in a meaningful way. However, it really is no more than many bishops expect of themselves in discerning the readiness of young people for confirmation. Whatever process a bishop uses to assure himself of the readiness of the confirmation candidates can also be used with those he is about to declare "elect."

A sponsor walks with the catechumen only for the period of the catechumenate. A godparent makes a lifetime commitment. The catechumens are free to choose their sponsor to be their godparent if they wish, or they may choose someone else. That should be made clear to them early in their process. Note that like the catechumens, the godparents are also called by name in the ritual.

The first public action of the godparents is to give testimony to the community as to the readiness of the catechumens for election. This is a significant reason for having the sponsor also serve as the godparent because the sponsor would have been a front row observer of God's work in the life of the catechumen. If the godparent is someone other than the sponsor, the catechumen needs to choose someone who will be able to offer meaningful testimony.

SCRUTINIES

The next three rites are the scrutines, which are celebrated in the parish on the Third, Fourth, and Fifth Sundays of Lent.

U.S. parishes, in particular, can be a little uncomfortable with the scrutinies. Our sense of egalitarianism makes us ask who are we to question the faith life of these elect. Certainly we are no better than they are.

Well, of course we aren't. But that isn't the point of the scrutinies. The scrutinies are first of all pastoral in nature and meant to help the elect on their journey. The RCIA says:

> The scrutinies are meant
> to *uncover*, then *heal*
> all that is weak, defective, or sinful in the hearts of the elect;
> to *bring out*, then *strengthen*
> all that is upright, strong, and good.
> For the scrutinies are celebrated in order
> to *deliver* the elect from the power of sin and Satan,
> to *protect* them against temptation, and
> to *give them strength* in Christ,
> who is the way, the truth, and the life. (141, emphasis added)

Each of the scrutinies is intended to lead the elect into deeper and deeper reflection on the mystery of sin and its antidote, the power of Christ within them.

Regardless of the lectionary year, the readings from Year A are always used for the scrutinies.

First Scrutiny

The first scrutiny, celebrated on the Third Sunday of Lent, focuses on John's gospel story of the woman at the well. The elect hear of the woman's thirst and are led to ask what it is in their lives that is drying them out. What is it that would refresh and revive them? Where will they find this living water?

Second Scrutiny

The next Sunday, the elect hear the story of the man born blind. In this gospel, it is not only the man who is blind but also many of those in his community who are "blind" to Christ's power. While the elect must grapple with the forces of darkness in their own lives, they must also grapple with the darkness of the society in which they live.

Third Scrutiny

The final scrutiny, on the Fifth Sunday of Lent, focuses on sin's ultimate result—physical death. The elect must reconcile themselves to the call to die with Christ. If they can make that final leap of faith, then, like Lazarus, they will be raised. Death will have no more power over them. This is the most difficult of the three progressions, and we must surround the elect with our prayers and support so they will "deepen their resolve to hold fast to Christ" (141).

The elect must celebrate all three scrutinies if they are to be baptized. Long before Lent, you need to make sure they have no schedule conflicts that would prevent them from celebrating each of the three rites. If they have an unavoidable conflict with any of the scrutinies, that is a "discernment issue" about their readiness for the Rite of Election and baptism this year. Each of the three scrutinies is **that** *important. If something unavoidable arises* **after** *the Rite of Election, you must ask the bishop to formally dispense the elect from celebrating the scrutiny in question. (See paragraph 20.)*

INTERCESSIONS IN THE SCRUTINIES

Open your RCIA to paragraph 153 (and flip over to 167 and 174). Note the rubric that reads, "the intentions may be adapted to fit various circumstances."

So, of course, you will want to compose intercessions that reflect the circumstances of the elect who will actually be celebrating the rite.

How do you know what the various circumstances of the elect are? That should be part of your ongoing discernment process during the lenten period. Before each scrutiny, spend some time with the elect in prayerful reflection. Each week, focus the reflection on

- what the elect thirst for,
- what blinds them and the world around them,
- and what they need to die to.

Based on their reflections, write prayers asking God to

- quench their thirst,
- enlighten them,
- and save them from death.

PREPARING THE ELECT

The preparation of the elect for the scrutinies is a spiritual preparation. According to the RCIA, "the elect must have the intention of achieving an intimate knowledge of Christ and his Church, and they are expected particularly to progress in genuine self-knowledge through serious examination of their lives and true repentance" (142).

The characters in the gospel stories for the Third, Fourth, and Fifth Sundays of Lent (Year A) are the models of how to accomplish this intimacy and self-knowledge. Your job and the job of the catechumenate team and the godparents is to help the elect remain focused on their spiritual progress throughout the weeks of Lent.

Catholics are already well acquainted with the lenten disciplines of prayer, fasting, and almsgiving (charity). In order to assist the elect in their spiritual growth, the catechumenate team and the godparents will want to be exemplary in their practice of these disciplines.

The *Catechism of the Catholic Church* is even more explicit in describing ways we can exhibit a penitential discipline. Your catechumenate team might reflect on these practices (and even list others) and choose several to be particularly diligent about during the coming Lent. You would, of course, encourage and exhort the elect to follow your example. These are some of the practices listed in the *Catechism*:

- gestures of reconciliation
- concern for the poor
- the exercise and defense of justice and right (cf. Amos 5:24; Isaiah 1:17)
- the admission of faults to one's brothers and sisters
- fraternal correction
- revision of life
- examination of conscience
- spiritual direction
- acceptance of suffering
- endurance of persecution for the sake of righteousness
- taking up one's cross each day and following Jesus
- reading Scripture
- praying the liturgy of the hours
- praying the Lord's Prayer (1436-1437)

In addition to this, the scrutinies themselves are meant to lead the elect to deeper intimacy with Christ and genuine self-knowledge. They will have a more profound experience of the scrutinies if you provide a time of reflection for them beforehand and afterward.

Schedule some time during the week before each scrutiny to reflect on the Scriptures for the rites, particularly the gospels. Lead the elect in a guided faith-sharing process (similar to what you might have experienced in a RENEW group or on a Cursillo), exploring the progression of faith and trust in the characters in the stories. This reflection could also lead to the crafting of the intercessions for the scrutinies we spoke of above.

Follow each scrutiny with a mystagogical reflection on their experience of the rite. The impact of the rite will be more profound and the mystagogical reflection richer if the elect are not overly concerned before the rite about what they have to do. In other words, avoid "rehearsing" the elect. Let them experience the rite as it unfolds.

On the other hand, the rite is not a secret. It's okay to share details about what will take place if some of the elect are particularly anxious. But listen closely to what they are asking about. Usually they only need a general description, not a detailed account of every aspect of the rite. The elect should not be at a rehearsal or walkthrough of the rite. That is the job of the liturgy team and the job of the godparents.

Minor rites

During Lent, you may also celebrate the Presentation of the Creed and the Presentation of the Lord's Prayer. These presentations might also be celebrated before Lent, during the catechumenate period (147-149). For a ritual outline for celebrating the presentations, go to TeamRCIA.com.

On Holy Saturday, the RCIA advises that you bring the elect and their godparents (and other members of the parish) together to celebrate the Recitation of the Creed and the Ephphetha Rite. You also have the option of presenting the Lord's Prayer on Holy Saturday. For an outline for a day of reflection for the elect, go to TeamRCIA.com.

 The preparation rites on Holy Saturday also include the Rite of Choosing a Baptismal Name. However, in the United States, the U.S. bishops have said that the elect are to be baptized using their given names (33.4). You might spend some time on Holy Saturday having the elect tell the story of how their parents named them or what their name has meant to them.

REFLECTION

The type of reflection that we focus on with the elect is mystagogical reflection. I often encounter folks in ministry who are mystified by the word "mystagogy."

Let's just demystify it right now. All it is, really, is a reflection on the mystery of God's love.

It is simple, but also vital. Mystagogical reflection helps us see what happened to us when we realized we had an encounter with God. It's like talking with a friend about a movie. Sometimes we don't really absorb the full impact of a movie until after we've talked about it—and if you're a movie buff, you really talk about it. You talk about the cinematography, the plot, the directing, and all the subtle symbolism throughout the film. And there are those powerfully deep movies that we might see several times because they reveal deeper and deeper meaning each time we see them.

Mystagogy is simply the process of exploring that same kind of depth of meaning based on an encounter with God. In the period of purification and enlightenment, the mystagogical reflection is focused primarily on the central element of the formation of the elect—the rites. After the Rite of Election and each of the scrutinies, it is essential to provide an in-depth mystagogical reflection on the experience of the elect.

The fourth stage of the RCIA process is identified as the period of mystagogy. However, the process of mystagogical reflection is not limited to that stage. Mystagogical reflection happens throughout the process, beginning in the inquiry stage.

Mystagogical reflection has three steps:

1. Remembering
2. Discovering truth
3. Commitment to mission

Your reflection on the rites of the elect will necessarily follow that three-step process.

Remembering

If your reflection is taking place on a day other than when the rite was celebrated, do a short guided meditation recalling the highpoints of the liturgy.

Invite the elect to recall something in the liturgy that was especially powerful or moving. Ask them simply to name it, not to explain it.

Ask them to recall how they felt at that moment. Be sure to have them report *emotions,* not explanations.

Discovering truth

That moment they remember is an encounter with God. In that moment, God is revealing a truth to the elect that may not yet be fully realized in them. Ask them questions similar to these to try to bring the learning into their consciousness:

- What did (the thing you remember) tell you about God?
- What did (the thing you remember) tell you about Jesus?
- What did (the thing you remember) tell you about the church?
- What did (the thing you remember) tell you about our community?
- What did (the thing you remember) tell you about yourself as a disciple?

Commitment to mission

This is the big "so what?" If the elect have had a memorable encounter with the mystery of God's love, and if they have discovered a deeper truth about that reality, what difference will it make in their lives? Ask them questions like, "John, if you really think it is true that God [or Jesus, the church, the community, you] is like that, what does that mean for your life after you are baptized? How will you be different? How will people know that you are different?"

RETREATS

If you've got your RCIA handy, take a look at paragraph 139: "This is a period of more intense spiritual preparation, consisting more in interior reflection than in catechetical instruction…."

Here is a giant clue about how to structure this period. Instruction, *no.* Interior reflection, *yes.* Because the period of purification and enlightenment coincides with Lent, your parish is probably involved in many retreat-like activities during the lenten season. Perhaps some of these are:

- More intense prayer, both at church and at home
- Fasting

- A focus on charity
- Days of reflection
- Reconciliation services
- Lenten Bible study or faith-sharing groups
- Sunday homilies focused on renewal
- Other things not listed here?

If, with the help of their godparents, you immerse the elect in the normal lenten activity of the parish, you will have accomplished most of the retreat aspects of their preparation.

Once their lenten preparation is concluded, the elect are initiated at the Easter Vigil. More about that later. For the moment, let's look at the next stage on their journey, the period of mystagogy. Once the elect are initiated and move into this stage, they are called *neophytes*.

BONUS POINTS

If you want to go the extra mile with lenten retreats, schedule three parishwide days (or evenings) of reflection based on the gospel readings for Cycle A of the Third, Fourth, and Fifth Sundays of Lent (the woman at the well, the man born blind, and the raising of Lazarus). For an outline for an evening lenten reflection, go to TeamRCIA.com.

7
Stage Four: Mystagogy

A mystagogical process is used throughout the preparation of the catechumens. The final period of the process is called the period of mystagogy as a way of emphasizing that the ordinary life of the baptized person is mystagogical.

Open your RCIA to paragraph 244, and read how the rite describes this period:

> This is a time
> > for the community
> > and the neophytes [the newly baptized] together
> to grow
> > in deepening their grasp of the paschal mystery
> > and in making it part of their lives
> > > through meditation on the gospel,
> > > sharing in the Eucharist,
> > > and doing the works of charity.

I read that, and I wonder, so what is the rest of our life supposed to be about? It seems like the period of mystagogy is the same as the rest of Christian life.

Exactly!

The period of mystagogy is a kind of refresher course for *both* the community and the neophytes. It is not any different from the ordinary Christian life. It is simply an intensified remembering of what we, the baptized, are to be about every day of the year.

HOW DO WE GET THEM TO COME BACK?

A complaint I often hear from catechumenate teams is they have difficulty getting the neophytes to come back for mystagogy. It is true that some number of those baptized at the Easter Vigil do not remain active in their parishes. People give lots of different estimates about how many, but the truth is, no one knows for sure. No one has ever done a systematic count of how many do not return.

However, there are not as many "dropouts" as you might think. Many of the newly baptized do continue to participate in Sunday Mass, even if many do not continue to participate in weekly meetings with catechists and godparents. We cannot consider these folks inactive. The Sunday liturgy is where they should be. If they are there, that's good news.

But what about those who really do drop out, even from Sunday liturgy? Sometimes we tend to blame them and say things like, we told them this was a lifelong commitment, and, we told them community life was central to Catholicism, and, we told them this was *initiation*, not *graduation*.

Other times we blame ourselves and say things like, I guess we didn't tell them enough, or, maybe we didn't tell them often enough, or, maybe we didn't go into enough detail.

Either response is missing the point. Both are based on an assumption that our job in the catechumenate is to give the catechumens good information. While good information is important, that's not our job. Our job is conversion. Like Calvin's transmogrifer, the RCIA is all about conversion. If the neophytes are not remaining committed, it is because their conversion was weak or non-existent.

Conversion never happens by giving out good information. Conversion happens when the Holy Spirit quickens the heart of a seeker and the Christian community surrounds that person with love. Conversion happens through relationship, not education.

POSTBAPTISMAL CATECHESIS

This period is also called the Period of Postbaptismal Catechesis. If you still have your RCIA open, flip over to paragraph 247. You'll see there that the main setting for the postbaptismal catechesis of this period is the Sunday Masses of the Easter season. If the Sunday Masses of Easter are the central place of mystagogy, what does the catechesis look like? Here is a list of essential elements for effective postbaptismal catechesis:

- *An environment of hospitality* in which strangers and visitors are welcomed as warmly as long-time parishioners and old friends. (The neophytes learn to love the least among us.)

- *A variety of liturgical ministers* fulfilling the roles of the liturgy in a competent and grace-filled manner. (The neophytes learn that the body of Christ has many parts and many charisms.)

- *Joyful and uplifting music* that everyone can and does sing with gusto. (The neophytes learn the reign of God is an experience of joy and hope.)

- *Readings from Scripture* that proclaim the truth of Jesus, dead and risen, and what that means for the world. This is especially powerful in Cycle A. (The neophytes learn more deeply that they were baptized into Christ's death and are now heirs to eternal life.)

- *Homilies that recall the cosmic symbols of the Easter experience*, remind us we are a communion of saints, reconnect us with our ancient story of faith, exhort us to live that faith vibrantly, and thrill us with a vision of the fullness of God's reign, embodied in the neophytes and in the worshiping community. (The neophytes learn…well, everything.)

- *Bread that tastes like bread and abundant wine* that are consecrated by the full, conscious, and active participation of both the royal and the ordained priesthood and changed by the power of the Holy Spirit into the body and blood of Christ. (The neophytes learn that it is through ordinary gifts of creation, the work of our hands, our offering of praise, and the holy order of the church that Christ becomes really and truly present.)

- *A dismissal into the world* that is understood by everyone not to be the end of Mass but the beginning of mission. (The neophytes learn that their preparation period has come to a close and now they must go out and do what they promised to do.)

Meetings other than Sunday Mass

Many parishes already have an ongoing adult faith formation process. In those parishes using a process similar to Generations of Faith or whole community catechesis, the entire parish is involved in a regular mystagogical reflection on the Sunday readings and liturgies. It would be very natural for the godparents of the neophytes to bring them to these sessions.

In parishes that do not have ongoing adult faith formation, the neophytes might be invited to gather during the weeks of Easter to reflect on all that has happened to them. This might be just the neophytes and their godparents, or it might be a broader group that includes catechumens and members of the parish.

It is beneficial to have at least one meeting, shortly after the Easter Vigil, to reflect mystagogically on the events of the Vigil.

The RCIA also suggests a meeting with the bishop and the neophytes along with a celebration of the Eucharist at which the bishop presides (see 251).

In addition, April and May are usually active times in the parish. Prepare the godparents ahead of time to make sure the neophytes are involved in a wide range of the parish activities.

In every case, however, these gatherings should be thought of as supplemental. The Sunday liturgy is the primary gathering for the neophytes.

Some parishes have gotten the idea that the period of mystagogy is a time to sign the neophytes up for parish ministries. This is a misunderstanding of the purpose of this period. The neophytes will, of course, have been involved in many ministries of the parish over the course of their catechumenate because the ministries of the parish are a part of their apprenticeship in the Christian life. If, after their baptism, they feel drawn to a particular ministry within the parish, then direct them to the right place to get more information. Resist the urge, however, to see these new Christians as fresh recruits for parish committees. Their primary ministry is in the world, witnessing to their new faith.

8 Lifelong Formation

The period of mystagogy lasts for fifty days as a formal, structured time of postbaptismal catechesis. In the United States, the bishops have asked that for a longer, less structured time, the parish pay particular attention to the neophytes, integrating them more deeply into the life of the parish. Open your RCIA, and flip to "Appendix III: National Statutes for the Catechumenate," paragraph 24:

> After the immediate mystagogy
> or postbaptismal catechesis
> during the Easter season,
> the program for the neophytes should extend until
> the anniversary of Christian initiation,
> with at least monthly assemblies of the neophytes
> for their deeper Christian formation and incorporation
> into the full life of the Christian community.

If the RCIA is about converting the catechumens, the life of the parish is about forming Catholics. The U.S. bishops wrote in *Our Hearts Were Burning Within Us: A Pastoral Plan for Adult Faith Formation in the United States*:

> Before us, in the wonder of God's gracious plan, stretch new opportunities to proclaim the Good News of Jesus to all the world. We are eager to witness and share the word of life about the reign of God faithfully, so that each new generation can hear this word in its own accents and discover Christ as its Savior.

Every disciple of the Lord Jesus shares in this mission. To do their part, adult Catholics must be mature in faith and well equipped to share the Gospel, promoting it in every family circle, in every church gathering, in every place of work, and in every public forum. They must be women and men of prayer whose faith is alive and vital, grounded in a deep commitment to the person and message of Jesus. (1-2)

The reason a parish exists is to form disciples to do the mission. Like the catechumenate, this formation happens not primarily by dispensing information but by building relationships. In *Our Hearts Were Burning*, the bishops describe how to build those relationships in a way that leads to mission success. The bishops offer ten criteria for discerning the lifelong formation process in a parish. Use this checklist to test how well your parish forms the neophytes during their mystagogical year through the relationships they foster in the community:

1. How are people encouraged to examine their basic assumptions about life and its ultimate meaning?

2. How do they acquire the perspective and skills for an intelligent appropriation of Catholic Christian tradition and an honest, informed assessment of contemporary culture?

3. How is the Christian message lived, communicated, and explored?

4. How do people experience Christian community in family, parish, small groups, and ecumenical encounters?

5. How do they actively participate in liturgical, small group, family, and personal prayer?

6. How are they involved in assessing local needs and discerning pastoral priorities?

7. How is Christian stewardship in parish and society called forth and welcomed?

8. How do they personally serve the "least ones" (Mt 25:45)?

9. How are they involved in shaping public policy and making society more just?

10. In short, how is learning in faith already happening through the ordinary experience of parish life and mission? (122)

PART THREE

THE RITES OF THE CATECHUMENATE

9 First Class Passage on the Journey of Faith

The heart of the catechumenate is the rites. The very name of the enterprise is *Rite* of Christian Initiation of Adults. All the activity of the catechumenate process is meant to flow from and lead back to the liturgy. The normative formation event for the catechumens is the Sunday assembly. However, at certain points on their journey, the catechumens participate in specific rituals that move them from one stage to another.

Think of the rites as doorways the candidates travel through to get from one period to the next:

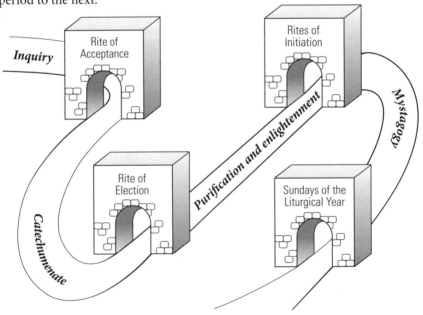

LIFELONG FORMATION

10 Rite of Acceptance

ou're going to need your RCIA text for this section. Open it to paragraph 41 and read through it carefully. Note this important point: The inquirers who are candidates for the catechumenate are assembling publicly for the first time.

In liturgy-language, a public assembly is extremely important. The inquirers, at the moment they assemble publicly, are no longer a group of individuals seeking to become Catholic. They are a community, formed for mission. Their public assembly is their first act of ministry. At that moment, before the liturgy even formally begins, they have been transformed ("transmogrified") into liturgical symbols. Sometimes catechumenate teams are concerned about shy candidates who may not want to participate in such a public ritual. The candidates' willingness to make a public declaration of faith is a factor in the discernment of their readiness. If they are not ready to assemble publicly for this ritual, they may not be ready to enter into the catechumenate.

There are two reasons to have them assemble publicly:

1. to declare their intentions to become members of the church;

2. for the church, in turn, to accept them into the formal process of becoming members.

WHEN THE RITE TAKES PLACE

The Rite of Acceptance can take place on almost any Sunday of the year. Some Sundays, however, are better than others. Consider these three factors when scheduling the Rite of Acceptance:

1. the readiness of the candidates
2. possible conflicts with the rest of the parish schedule
3. the liturgical focus of the given Sunday

 For a list of suggested Sundays that have an appropriate liturgical focus for each current liturgical year, see Appendix 5.

Ideally, a parish would choose two to four possible Sundays on which to celebrate the Rite of Acceptance in the coming year. When one of the Sundays begins to approach, the parish would discern the readiness of the inquirers to move to the next stage. If none of the candidates are ready, the Sunday is simply celebrated as usual in the parish.

PLANNING THE RITE

Before you begin planning the rite (paragraphs 48-68) you need to read the entire rite through, beginning to end. Underline things you want to remember, make notes in the margins, use Post-Its.

Remote preparation

After you have read through the rite, go to the church when it's empty and walk through the rite yourself.

RECEIVING THE CANDIDATES

The first action is to gather with the candidates and their sponsors outside the church (48). (Remember that when a rite talks about "candidates," it does not mean "baptized candidates" but candidates for the rite.) Will you gather the assembly outside or gather inside and then go outside? Where will the candidates and sponsors be standing? Where will the assembly stand? Imagine the assembly and how well they can see and hear in that configuration. As you walk through each part of the rite, keep imagining yourself as a candidate or as a person in the assembly. Have you put them in the best possible place at every part of the rite?

Greeting

The greeting is informal. You can adapt this to involve the catechetical director if that seems appropriate. Even though it is informal, the greeting should be written out ahead of time. It should be very brief.

Opening dialogue

The purpose of the dialogue is for the community to meet ritually for the first time those who want to become part of God's church. The dialogue should be spontaneous, not formulaic. Instead of the rather cold: "What is your name" given in the ritual text, ask the sponsors to introduce the candidates to the community.

Imagine how long the sponsors will need to speak. Imagine how loud they will have to be. Will you need an amplification system? If so, make a note.

Now look at paragraph 50. Then skip down to the long paragraph that starts, "The celebrant continues with the following questions…." Note the second sentence, which reads: "The celebrant may use other words than those provided in asking the candidates [for the Rite of Acceptance] about their intentions and may let them answer in their own words."

Use other words than those provided. Why would you want to do that? Because this is real life. You want to catechize both the candidates and the assembly that something powerful and important is taking place. The presider should ask a real question and expect to get a real answer. So the presider asks a real question: "John, what is it you are seeking?" What does John say?

Well, I don't want to put words in John's mouth, and neither should you. John should answer honestly about what he is seeking. If he doesn't know what he is seeking, he is not yet ready to become a catechumen.

John's entire time in the inquiry period should have focused on why he has come forward. What is it he is seeking? What does he want? Who moves him and calls him? After months of struggling with questions like these, John will be more than ready to give a real answer when the question is put to him in the ritual. And the assembly will recognize it for what it is—a statement of faith.

Candidates' first acceptance of the gospel

This part of the ritual sometimes gets confused with the later, optional, presentation of a Bible. "Gospel" means the message of Jesus—follow me, you must die to have new life, go and tell the good news. The purpose of this part of the ritual is to ask the candidates if they are willing to follow Jesus to the Cross.

Read the small print of paragraph 52 closely:

> The celebrant addresses the candidates, adapting one of the following formularies…*to the answers received in the opening dialogue.* (Emphasis added)

So suppose John Candidate is asked in the opening dialogue what he's seeking, and suppose he says something like: "I am looking for *peace and happiness* in my life." Using formulary A, paragraph 52, the presider might respond: "John, God gives *peace and happiness* to everyone who asks for it...." Or, adapting formulary B, he might say, "John, God is our Creator, and he created us to live in *peace and happiness*...." Or, using C: "John, this is *peace and happiness*: to know the one true God and Jesus Christ...."

The rite presumes the presider is addressing the candidates as a group. But it is more powerful to address the candidates individually. If you have a large number of candidates, consider dividing them among Mass times or even different Sundays so that the rite can be as powerful as possible.

At the conclusion of the dialogue with each candidate, the presider asks for a promise. Are you ready to start the journey? Are you ready to live this life? Are you ready to accept the Gospel? Are you ready to go to the cross? The presider can adapt the question to the individual, but it has to elicit a firm commitment to mission.

After each individual response, Yes! or I am!, sing an acclamation of joy. (Write this down in your preparation notes: "Ask music ministry to prepare acclamation.")

Affirmation by the sponsors and the assembly

Now it is time for the sponsors and the assembly to promise to help the candidates keep their promise. I always think the assembly gets a little shortchanged here. If you read the text (paragraph 53), they're thrown into the sentence as a parenthetical afterthought. It is more powerful to ask the sponsors first, get their reply, then ask the assembly.

After both the sponsors and the assembly have promised to help the candidates, and after the prayer of thanks that concludes this first part of the rite, sing an acclamation of joy. (You can use the same one from before; you don't want to tax the musicians!)

Signing of the candidates with the cross

The signing is a *huge* symbol in the rite. We cradle Catholics are so used to signing ourselves and anything in range of our thumbs that we tend to take the symbol for granted. It can seem ordinary and casual. This is the first time the candidates will be signed publicly, so we want to make sure they are *really* signed. We are going to make use of the optional "Signing of the Other Senses" (paragraph 56). (We'll say more about how that works in the rehearsal section.)

It is also important that the assembly can see and hear this part of the rite. So check in now with your imaginary assembly. Is there a better place for them to be standing? Should you have moved them there in the beginning when they first gathered? If so, write that down in your notes.

Sometimes the only configuration that will work is back inside the church. Some parishes that don't have a good place to gather outside the church will adapt the rite so that the candidates, sponsors, and assembly process in before the signings take place to let everyone see and hear better.

Invitation to the celebration of the Word of God

Imagine where the cross bearer, presider, catechumens, sponsors, and assembly are standing at the end of the concluding prayer. Where are the musicians? Where are you? What has to happen to make a smooth transition from outside to inside? Will you need hospitality ministers to open the doors? Will you need others to help guide the assembly? Walk through it in your head and make notes.

LITURGY OF THE WORD
Instruction and Readings

If you look at paragraph 61, the instruction is intended to be an explanation of the dignity of God's word. If you are celebrating this ritual at a Sunday liturgy, it would be difficult to justify adding more words at this point. You can accomplish the same goal by treating the lectionary with dignity and having the word proclaimed powerfully. Note that the rubrics suggest incensing it, for example. Make a note to schedule your best lectors for this celebration.

Homily

The homily should take into account the journey of the catechumens. Make a note to schedule some reflection time before the rite with the candidates and the homilist.

Presentation of a Bible

Note this is an optional part of the liturgy (indicated by the brackets around it in the ritual text; see paragraph 64). It is optional because, ideally, the catechumens will have been introduced to the Bible during their inquiry and may already have their own copy. The Bible will not be new to them. What will be new for them is the liturgical proclamation of Scripture. So the following slight adaptation to this ritual will make it much more meaningful for the catechumens.

After the homily, the sponsors escort the catechumens to a visible place in the assembly. Walk around the church, and think about where the best place may be. They don't have to all stay together. If you have more than a couple of catechumens, spread them out, perhaps in the aisles between the pews, so all the members of the assembly can see at least one catechumen close up.

While the catechumens are getting into place, the leader of the catechumenate team (or another member of the team) goes to the ambo to get the Book of Gospels or the lectionary. If that is not you, where will you need to be sitting to prompt her if she forgets? Make a note.

The leader processes the (open) gospel book to the first catechumen. The leader or the presider proclaims: "John, receive the Gospel of Jesus Christ." Then the sponsor places the catechumen's hand on the open book and says, "John, find in this word _____."

What goes in the blank? Whatever John said he was seeking when he was asked this question at the beginning of the rite. So if John said he was looking for *peace and happiness*, John's sponsor would say: "John, find in this word *peace and happiness*."

At this point, the musicians might lead the assembly in the same acclamation you sang outside when the catechumens first accepted the gospel. (Make a note for the musicians.) As the assembly sings, the leader moves to the next catechumen, and the process is repeated.

Consider having the catechumen kiss the Book of Gospels or the lectionary during the sung acclamation. It is another way to emphasize the dignity of God's word without a verbal explanation. Make a note to practice with the sponsors so they can direct their catechumens gracefully.

Intercessions for the catechumens

Don't simply default to the intercessions given in the rite. Spend some time writing intercessions that reflect the journey of the catechumens who will be celebrating this rite. Be sure the person who will proclaim them has them soon enough to spend time rehearsing them. Remember the assembly at this point. They will have been sitting since the homily and may not immediately realize they should stand. Make a note for the presider to gesture them up if necessary.

Prayer over the catechumens

The rite indicates that the presider extends his hands over the catechumens (66). You might adapt this to have everyone in the assembly extend their hands as well. If you think your parishioners would be comfortable enough, you might invite those standing nearby the catechumens actually to lay hands on the catechumens' heads and shoulders. Craft a sentence for the presider to introduce the prayer and give direction at the same time. Here some examples:

1. Let us extend our hands over our brothers and sisters and pray.

2. Let us extend hands or place our hands on our brothers and sisters and pray.

3. Let us place our hands on these catechumens or on those nearest to them as we pray.

DISMISSAL OF THE CATECHUMENS

The ritual usually takes place at a Sunday Mass, and so the catechumens are dismissed before the Liturgy of the Eucharist.

In some places, the dismissal of the catechumens is treated as though it were optional. It really isn't. If you look at paragraph 67c of the RCIA, the rule reads: "If for serious reasons the catechumens cannot leave…." The rite envisions that the catechumens are always dismissed except in rare circumstances. If you are planning to have the catechumens spread throughout the assembly for the presentation of the word, walk through how are you going to get them to process out as a group in the dismissal. They would be led by a catechist, carrying the Book of Gospels or lectionary, and the assembly would sing an acclamation (note to musicians).

Remember that the sponsors *do not* leave with the catechumens. For an outline of a 30-minute dismissal session, see the appendix.

Music is crucial to this rite. If you are not musical by nature, it would be good to sit down with a musician and talk through the entire rite together. Ask the musician to help you imagine creative ways music could enhance the rite and move it from one stage to the next. Think more of acclamations than full blown hymns.

Also, ask the musician to help you hear how some of the prayers might be sung. Pay particular attention to prayers the presider might chant a cappella. Some things that could be chanted include:

- *The invocations for the signings (paragraph 56)*
- *The concluding prayer after the signings (paragraph 57)*
- *The gospel (it is an ancient tradition for the deacon to chant the gospel)*
- *The intercessions*
- *The prayer over the catechumens (paragraph 66)*

11 Election or Enrollment of Names

The steps the catechumens take on their initiation journey are always public rituals. The first step was the Rite of Acceptance. The second step is the Rite of Election. It is also called the Rite of Enrollment because the catechumens write their names in the book that lists those who will be initiated. *Election* means *choice*.

WHEN THE RITE TAKES PLACE

The Rite of Election normally takes place on the First Sunday of Lent (126), and Lent serves as a time of spiritual preparation for the elect. For pastoral reasons, the rite may be celebrated in the week before or after the First Sunday of Lent. In most dioceses, the parish Rite of Sending is celebrated at one of the regular Sunday Masses and the Rite of Election is celebrated that afternoon at the cathedral.

It is possible to celebrate the Rite of Election at a time other than Lent, say in the fall. However, even though the rite allows it, it is rare. A parish would still need to enter a six-week "Lent-like" period before the elect could be initiated (126).

RITE OF SENDING CATECHUMENS FOR ELECTION

To fully grasp the pastoral sense of the election (choosing) of the catechumens, we have to hold two rituals in our head at the same time. The primary ritual, which is required of the catechumens to be baptized, is the Rite of Election. The Rite of Election is almost always celebrated at the cathedral and presided over by the bishop.

Because most of the parishioners, who have presumably been deeply involved in the formation of the catechumens for a long time, will not participate in the diocesan Rite of Election, the RCIA provides an optional parish celebration that looks like the Rite of Election in many ways, but its purpose is different. The Rite of Sending formally sends the catechumens to the bishop with the parish's testimonies of approval. The parish celebration takes place at one of the primary Masses on the First Sunday of Lent. In most parishes, elements of the diocesan Rite of Election are taken over into the parish celebration. Different dioceses have different customs, and you'll need to check with your diocesan liturgy office for final guidance on what you are able to adapt for your parish. I'm going to discuss the practice in most dioceses, and you'll need to flip back and forth in your RCIA text to follow along.

If you have both catechumens and candidates, you might use the alternate rite in the RCIA, Appendix I, 2. But many dioceses only celebrate a Rite of Election (with catechumens only) and not a combined Rite of Election and Call to Continuing Conversion (with both catechumens and candidates for full communion). If your diocese celebrates only the Rite of Election, it doesn't make sense to "send" the candidates for full communion to the bishop. In this section, we are going to focus on the catechumens. (The candidates for full communion will be dealt with in Appendix 3.)

Rite of Election

TESTIMONY

So let's start with a look at the Rite of Election. The principles of that rite will inform what you do in your parish's Rite of Sending. Open up your RCIA to paragraph 119. If you are looking at the paragraph closely, you will see the *key* to this rite. The election (choice) depends upon "the testimony of godparents and catechists and of the catechumens' reaffirmation of their intention...."

That is a *lot* of pressure on the godparents and the catechists! Are they able to testify honestly about God's work in the lives of the catechumens? Perhaps, without letting the godparents and catechists off the hook, we can at least help them feel less lonely. Given that the entire parish is responsible for forming the catechumens, we might also say the testimony of the parishioners is also essential. So, especially in the parish rite of sending, we might try to find a way to allow the assembly to testify as well.

Based on this testimony, the church chooses (elects) who will be baptized.

Presentation of the catechumens

The presentation is similar in both the Rite of Election and in the parish Rite of Sending. Turn to paragraph 130 (111 in the Rite of Sending) and note the wide flexibility allowed in this section of the rite. Since just about anyone in the parish is allowed to present the catechumens, you need to ask yourself who is the *right* person in your parish. In most cases, it is going to be the catechumenate team leader. He or she will have had the broadest and most constant contact with the catechumens, and it will seem right to the catechumens themselves that the team leader is the one standing up on their behalf.

> **A CHANGE IN RELATIONSHIP**
>
> There is a significant shift here in contrast to the Rite of Acceptance. In their first public gathering, the catechumens had to be introduced to the community. We did not know their names. Now, after all this time, we know them. We don't need to ask who has come before us as we did in the Rite of Acceptance. Now we call them forth by name.

Affirmation by the godparents [and the assembly]

The affirmation is also similar in both the Rite of Election and the Rite of Sending. However, in the parish rite, you will want to take full advantage of the permission to adapt ("in these or similar words," paragraph 112).

The presider addresses the godparents and asks them for their testimony about the catechumens. Instead of following that with a series of yes-or-no questions, prepare the godparents to offer actual testimony. For example: "Jane, can you testify to John's readiness to be presented to the bishop for the Rite of Election?"

At this point, Jane speaks from her heart about the way she has seen God work in John's life. (From her heart does not mean unprepared!) It is important that she make God the subject of her testimony. That is, have her start her testimony with "God has…." The temptation is to start with "John has…." John has participated in the formation sessions; John has come to church every Sunday; John has worked in the soup kitchen; John has been a great guy. The focus is in the wrong place. The testimony needs to be about how *God* has changed John's life and how *God* has made John ready.

Testimony is given for each catechumen. Then, depending on your particular parish and the time available, the presider might also ask if anyone in the assembly wishes to testify for any of the catechumens. This *is* more spontaneous than it is for the godparents. However, it shouldn't be a complete surprise to the assembly. The RCIA says, "On the day of election…the faithful, when called upon, should be sure to give honest and carefully considered testimony about the catechumens" (9.3). If you are not able to ask the assembly for testimony during the liturgy, you will want to explore other means for soliciting their input. (For suggestions on how to involve the assembly in "testifying," see TeamRCIA.com.)

Invitation and enrollment of names

At this point in the Rite of Election, the enrollment of names follows the testimonies. In the parish Rite of Sending, the catechumens are prayed over and dismissed. However, in many dioceses, the inscription of names takes place in the parish, not at the cathedral. If you aren't sure of the practice in your diocese, check with your diocesan worship office. For those of you who inscribe the names in your local parishes, you will need to write a simple text for the presider to speak. For example, "John, if your faith makes you ready, write your name in the Book of Life." The catechumens may write their names themselves or they may call out their names, which are then inscribed by the godparents or by the leader of the catechumenate team.

Prayer over the catechumens / Dismissal of the catechumens
In the Rite of Election, the actual election follows the enrollment of names. However, in the parish Rite of Sending, the catechumens would be prayed over (114-115) and dismissed (if Eucharist is to follow; 116). Note the rubric in paragraph 117 that the Creed and intercessions may be omitted from the liturgy if time is a factor.

12 Scrutinies

INTRODUCTION

Before we can talk about the scrutinies, we have to clear a few things up.

1. The scrutinies are celebrated *only* with the elect. There is no combined rite that includes the baptized candidates for full initiation.

2. Only the elect are scrutinized. Nothing in the liturgy should indicate that the baptized candidates or the assembly are also being scrutinized.

3. In fact, it is the assembly that *does the scrutinizing.*

If you turn to paragraph 141, you will see that the purpose of each of the scrutinies is "to uncover, then heal all that is weak" in the elect and "to bring out, then strengthen all that is…good." In the prayers of the rite, pay particular attention to words like *deliver, heal, strengthen,* and *free.*

WHEN THE RITE TAKES PLACE

Look at paragraph 146. Normally, the scrutinies take place on the Third, Fourth, and Fifth Sundays of Lent. If for some unusual reason the scrutinies cannot be celebrated on those Sundays, they can be celebrated on other lenten Sundays or even during a weekday. For really unusual reasons, the scrutinies might even be celebrated outside of Lent. But in that case, you would need to observe an entire "period of purification and enlightenment"—another 40 days similar to Lent.

Whenever the scrutinies are celebrated, the readings from the Third, Fourth, and Fifth Sundays of Lent, Year A, are always used.

PLANNING THE RITE

The structure of each of the three scrutinies is the same. However, the prayers reflect the three different gospels for the Third, Fourth, and Fifth Sundays of Lent. Be sure to give yourself plenty of time to carefully read through each scrutiny long before it is time to start planning. The scrutinies are found at paragraphs 150-156, 164-170, and 171-177. Underline, write in the margins, and use Post-Its to keep track of things you'll want to emphasize in your planning.

> When the scrutinies are celebrated, we **do not** use the prayers of the Masses for the Third, Fourth, and Fifth Sundays of Lent. Instead, the prayers for "Christian Initiation: The Scrutinies" are used. You'll find those in the back of the sacramentary in the section titled "Ritual Masses." See RCIA 146.

REMOTE PREPARATION

After you have read through the rite, go to the church and walk through the whole thing yourself.

Invitation to silent prayer

The scrutiny begins after the homily. The rite says that after the homily, the elect and their godparents come forward before the presider (152). Now think about that for a minute. If you are worshiping in a traditional-style church, altar up front with two sections of pews running a half-football field back to the door, most people are not going to be able to see the elect if you call them "forward." Think about where you want them to actually stand. If you have several elect, it might be better to disperse them throughout the assembly. Go and stand at various places in the church, and see how it feels to have the elect placed there.

Also, keep in mind the elect don't have a copy of the ritual in their hands. Even though the rite says they "come forward," there are no words in the text actually calling them forward. Make a note that during rehearsal you will have to emphasize to the godparents that it is their job to know when to stand and where to place the elect. The godparents can receive a nonverbal cue from you or from the presider. Or they can simply go to their places at the end of the homily.

Also note that no text is given for the presider's first addresses to the assembly (152). Make a note to either prepare a text for the presider or point out to him that he will need to prepare something.

He next addresses the elect, and again, no text is given. What's going on here? Why so much talking with so little scripting? It's clear the rite intends for these addresses to be "from the heart." That doesn't mean the presider's comments should be casual. When the presider speaks to both the elect and the assembly, he is inviting them to silent prayer. His remarks should be crafted in that context—brief, explicit, and solemn.

Generally, parish assemblies in the U.S. are not comfortable with the kind of profound silence the rite expects at this point. How long should this silence be? It is difficult to give absolutes, but it should be long enough that the assembly *feels* the silence. It is more than a pause. It is a long, deep look at the Holy. It is a gathering of courage and will before entering into a struggle with darkness.

The presider's remarks need to call the assembly to a silence that prepares them for this ritual. So, for example, once the godparents have brought their elect to their assigned places, the presider might say something like:

> Brothers and sisters, these elect before us have entered into a profound spiritual journey. As a sign of our solidarity with them, [let us stand and] hold them in silent and fervent prayer.

Note that the rite has the assembly stand *after* the silent prayer. However, there seems to be a greater sense of solemnity when the assembly is standing in silence, so you might consider making that adaptation.

The presider concludes his remarks with the words: "Elect of God, bow your heads [kneel down] and pray" (152). Imagine where the elect are standing and if you will have them bow or kneel. Try both postures yourself, and see how they feel. Kneeling certainly communicates the profound and solemn nature of this moment in a way that simply bowing one's head does not. If you are going to have them kneel, make a note to ask the godparents if any of the elect have physical limitations that would prevent them from doing so. Also, if you'll need to have cushions available (how was it for you when you knelt on the floor of the church?), make a note of that.

Should the assembly kneel?

I have been at scrutiny rites in which the assembly was also asked to kneel. There seems little justification for this. Perhaps we are embarrassed to pray so profoundly and deeply for the elect. But it is the elect who are being scrutinized, not the assembly. The very next action in the ritual is that the assembly prays for the elect. The traditional stance for intercession is standing, and that would be the appropriate posture for the assembly.

The place for the baptized candidates during the scrutiny is with the rest of the baptized, praying for the elect.

Intercessions for the elect

The rite presumes that both the assembly and the elect are standing for the intercessions. However, since these are prayers for the elect, you might adapt the rite so the elect remain kneeling (or remain with their heads bowed). The intercessions given in the text are merely models and should not be used verbatim. Make a note to adapt the intercessions to fit the "various circumstances" of the elect. (For suggestions on how to make these adaptations to the intercessions, go to TeamRCIA.com.)

The way the intercessions are proclaimed should receive as much attention as the proclamation of the Scriptures. Consider having them sung, and make a note to consult with the musicians.

Exorcism

Exorcism has two meanings, and it is difficult to focus on the correct one. The wrong meaning for the RCIA is the Linda-Blair-possessed-by-the-devil-scary-movie version. (That's the one you were thinking of, wasn't it?!)

The baptismal meaning is a lot better. In the initiation rites, an exorcism is a recognition that there is evil in the world. The "worldly," because they don't fully recognize or accept the power of Christ, are more susceptible to the power of evil than are the baptized. A baptismal exorcism is a prayer that the unbapitzed will be liberated from the power of evil and freed by the power of Christ. Even those of us who have been baptized since infancy have experienced an exorcism. It is a prayer prayed for babies in the Rite of Baptism. The prayer prayed in the scrutiny is longer but of the same nature. The word *exorcism* is never used in the prayer itself, and there is no reason to emphasize the word with the elect or the godparents. Emphasize instead the effect of the prayer.

The RCIA defines *exorcism* this way:

In the rite of exorcism…, the elect,
>who have already learned from the Church as their mother
>the mystery of deliverance from sin by Christ,
are freed
>from the effects of sin
>and from the influence of the devil.
They receive new strength
>in the midst of their spiritual journey
>and they open their hearts
>to receive the gifts of the Savior. (144, emphasis added)

Take a moment to read through the exorcism prayers again (154, 168, 175). As you read, underline the verbs that ask God to do something. Verbs like *protect, quench, stand, rule, show, stir up,* and most especially, *free.*

The prayer to free the elect from everything that holds them bound to an old way of living is the very climax of the entire scrutiny. As you are standing in the church, imagine the elect in the midst of the assembly. Are they still kneeling? Are they standing? Go and stand where the presider will be standing and imagine you are asking God to free the elect. What would your body posture be like? How would your voice sound? Try reading the prayer out loud. Try singing it. Emphasize the verb *free.* How will you communicate to the presider the powerful nature of this prayer? How will you communicate it to the assembly? And, most important, how will you communicate it to the elect?

Walk to the elect

As is the case with most of us, the elect will remember what is done to them more than what is said to them. In the middle of the exorcism prayer, there is a direction for the presider to lay hands on the elect. Physically walk to each spot where you intend each elect to be and imagine laying your hands on them. Kneel or stand where the elect will be. Place your own hands on your head and imagine the presider laying hands on your head.

Consider asking the catechumenate team leader to follow the presider and also lay hands on each of the elect. If you make that adaptation, then ask the godparents to lay hands on their individual candidates as well. The elect will then have a powerful, nonverbal experience of prayer that they will remember for a lifetime. Note that you will need to rehearse this well so it goes smoothly.

Walk back to the presider's chair

After the laying on of hands, the presider returns to his place and stretches out his hands for the remainder of the exorcism prayer. Will you have him invite the assembly to extend their hands as well? If so, make a note so you don't forget.

The exorcism prayer concludes with a song of thanksgiving. If your presider is musical, you might have him sing the exorcism prayer and have his song lead directly into the assembly's song. Use the psalms listed at the end of the prayer as guidance for the kind of song to choose at this point. (Psalms 32 and 40 are especially appropriate.) Choose *one* song or psalm that will work for each scrutiny in order to enhance the participation of the assembly in the singing. Make a note to consult with the musicians.

The exorcism prayer is Trinitarian. It begins with an address to God. That is followed by a laying on of hands, a traditional invocation of the Spirit. Finally, the prayer concludes by calling on Jesus to free the Elect and heal them.

Dismissal of the elect

At the conclusion of the exorcism prayer, if the elect are still kneeling, the godparents will assist them to stand. The elect remain wherever you have placed them in the assembly, and the presider dismisses them. A catechist or another minister (make a note to decide who on your team) exits carrying the Book of Gospels or lectionary. The godparents may need to guide the elect, who may be a little disoriented at this point, to follow the book. Make a rehearsal note. (The godparents *do not* leave; they remain in the assembly.)

Imagine how they will leave. Will they depart in silence? Will you sing an acclamation? Perhaps the refrain of the thanksgiving song you have just completed? Make a note to consult with the musicians.

Preparing the godparents

Besides being good examples at living a lenten lifestyle, an essential role for the godparents is to know the rite well enough to guide the elect through it. (The elect are not at the rehearsal.) You will need to schedule a time for a walkthrough close enough to the day of the ritual that the godparents can remember all the essential moments. The Saturday preceding the Sunday is usually a good time.

> When you have elect who are children, the parents may certainly stand with the godparents throughout the rite and share in the support of their children as they go through the liturgy.

For the scrutinies, the godparents have four critical moments to be aware of:

1. Before the rite, they need to pick up the elect from home or arrange to meet them at the door of the church before the liturgy. From that moment, they need to keep a hand on the elect at all times as an anchor of support.

2. After the homily, the godparents need to move the elect into the pre-assigned positions in the midst of or in front of the assembly.

3. During the exorcism, they may lay hands on the elect if you have adapted that part of the rite.

4. After the exorcism, if the elect are still kneeling, the godparents help the elect to their feet and guide them to follow the minister out of the church when they are dismissed.

None of these are complicated, but most godparents will be nervous. It is important to rehearse with them enough that they are able to quell their nerves and project a face of calm confidence for the elect.

> The pastoral reality is that not all godparents are chosen for their spiritual depth. Sometimes they are chosen because they are friends or family members, but they may be barely practicing Christians themselves. In those cases, you might want to consider having the sponsor from the catechumenate period or another team member stand with the godparent throughout the rites. In effect, the team member is godparenting the godparent who is godparenting the candidate.

13 Minor Rites

PRESENTATION OF THE CREED AND THE LORD'S PRAYER

Open your RCIA text to paragraph 147, and note the pastoral motivation for presenting the Creed and the Lord's Prayer to the elect. The church lovingly entrusts these ancient texts to the elect because they "have always been regarded as expressing the heart of the Church's faith and prayer." Each text provides the elect with deeper insight into faith:

The Creed,
    as it recalls the wonderful deeds of God
    for the salvation of the human race,
suffuses the vision of the elect
    with the sure light of faith.
The Lord's Prayer
    fills them with a deeper realization
    of the new spirit of adoption
        by which they will call God their Father,
        especially in the midst of the eucharistic assembly.

When the rites take place

The RCIA offers two options for celebrating the presentations.

1. The normal option is to celebrate the presentations in Lent, probably at a weekday Mass or during a day of reflection. (The Creed would be presented sometime after the first scrutiny and the Lord's Prayer after the third scrutiny.) (148-149)

2. However, the RCIA also allows the presentations to be celebrated during the catechumenate period "because the period of purification and enlightenment is rather short…" (104).

So how do you know which option to choose? It's a little complicated.

- If you have a year-round process (which all of us are working toward, right?),
- and if the presentations are celebrated in the catechumenate period,
- you wouldn't necessarily celebrate the presentations with all the catechumens.

The rite assumes you have some catechumens who are going to be baptized at the coming Easter Vigil and some who are going to remain in the process at least until the *next* Easter Vigil. In that case, the rite is telling us that the presentations would only take place "when the catechumens are judged ready for these celebrations" (104).

So you could either celebrate the presentations in Lent, or you could celebrate them during the catechumenate period with those catechumens who are most likely to be elected for initiation at the coming Easter Vigil. When you discern they are ready for the Rite of Election, then they are ready to celebrate the presentations. This second option seems to be the better of the two.

WHY CELEBRATE THE PRESENTATIONS EARLY?

Why would you want to celebrate the presentations early, before Lent? There are two reasons. First, as the rite suggests, Lent is short, and it is already overcrowded with lots of parish activity. The presentations can get a little lost in the shuffle. If you celebrate the presentations in Ordinary Time, you can integrate them into the Sunday Masses instead of weekday Masses. This allows a much larger portion of your primary team member—the parish community—to participate in the celebration with the catechumens.

The second reason is that by presenting the Creed and the Lord's Prayer in the catechumenate stage, they will have these central statements of the faith to help them enter into the lenten process more deeply from the first day of Lent.

 If you do celebrate the rites in the catechumenate stage, you'll need to edit the ritual texts, substituting the term "catechumens" for the term "elect."

Planning the rites

Before you begin planning the rites (paragraphs 157-163 and 178-184) you need to read through them, beginning to end. Underline things you want to remember, make notes in the margins, use Post-Its.

Preparing yourself

Let's assume you are going to celebrate these rituals during the catechumenate stage, probably during two Sunday Masses in winter Ordinary Time. First, check the parish calendar to see which Sundays are available. You don't want to celebrate the Presentation of the Creed at the same Mass that the Panikowskis are celebrating their fiftieth wedding anniversary with a renewal of vows!

Then read through the lectionary for the Sundays available, and choose one Sunday that is appropriate for the Presentation of the Creed and one that is appropriate for the Presentation of the Lord's Prayer.

Go to church

Next, go over to the church, and walk through the rites yourself. After the homily, the catechumens will be called forward. Who will call them? You? Another member of the team? The deacon? The presider? Make a note.

And where will they go once they are called forward? If you have several catechumens, consider placing them throughout the assembly. As with the other rituals, it will be the responsibility of the sponsors to know where the catechumens are to stand and to guide them there.

PRESENTATION OF THE CREED

Apostles' Creed or the Nicene Creed—which one do you choose?

Since the Nicene Creed is the one that we use in Mass every Sunday, that is probably the better option. The RCIA envisions that the handing over of the Creed is oral. There is no giving of a "scroll" or written text. Imagine where each catechumen is facing. Imagine where the assembly is facing. Will the presider need to verbally ask the assembly to face the catechumens or will they do so naturally? Make a note.

Then "hear" how the assembly will speak the Creed. You will want them to speak much more slowly and deliberately than they usually do. How will you get them to slow down and stay in unison? One option is to punctuate phrases of the Creed with a tone from a singing bowl, a hand bell, or a triangle. A tone to stop, another to begin again. Make a note to consult with the musicians. Or instruct the assembly to take a breath after each line.

PRESENTATION OF THE LORD'S PRAYER

The ritual text has the Presentation of the Lord's Prayer taking place as part of the Gospel proclamation. This arrangement assumes you are celebrating the rite during a weekday in Lent and not at a Sunday Mass. If you are celebrating the rite during a winter Sunday Ordinary Time Mass, you will have to adapt the ritual to look more like the structure used for the Presentation of the Creed. The gospel of the Sunday must be used and will not be Matthew's rendition of the Lord's Prayer. So move the presentation of the Lord's Prayer to after the homily.

Follow the same walkthrough procedure used for the Presentation of the Creed. As with the Creed, the handing over would be done orally in a slow and deliberate fashion.

PRAYER OVER THE CATECHUMENS

At the end of each presentation, there is prayer over the elect (or, if celebrating early, the catechumens). Consider having the presider invite the assembly to extend their hands over the candidates for the prayer. Note that the prayer includes the names of the candidates. Make sure the presider knows them or has a list.

DISMISSAL

Assuming this ritual is taking place at a Sunday Mass, the catechumens would be dismissed in the usual way.

There is an optional ritual on Holy Saturday during which the elect "return" the Creed to the community by reciting it from memory. See paragraph 193.

Preparing the sponsors

The sponsors will need a brief walkthrough, and the rehearsal of both rituals can be done together. The sponsors will be responsible for three things in both rituals:

1. They need to pick up the catechumens from home and bring them to church or meet them at the entrance before Mass begins.

2. They need to know the spot to direct the catechumens to, and they need to know the cue for moving them there.

3. They may need to prompt the catechumens to follow the dismissal minister since they may be standing in places they are not accustomed to.

PREPARATION RITES ON HOLY SATURDAY
Introduction

Turn to paragraph 185, and you will see there is only one thing that is *required* of the elect on Holy Saturday. It is to be a day of reflection and fasting. They are to refrain from their usual activities and spend the day in prayer.

The parish might gather the elect together for this day of prayer, providing space on the parish grounds or going away someplace. If you are able to bring the elect together, even for an hour or two, the rite suggests you celebrate some or all of the following:

- the presentation of the Lord's prayer if this has not already been done
- the "return" or recitation of the Creed from memory
- the ephphetha rite
- the choosing of a baptismal name

Planning the rites

Decide where you will celebrate the rites. You don't necessarily need to be in the church for these. Since the number of participants will be smaller than a Sunday assembly, a more intimate space may serve the rituals better.

You will also need to decide who will preside. The pastor is an obvious choice, but he might be busy with other tasks on Holy Saturday. A deacon could preside and so could the leader of the catechumenate team or another team member.

Preparing yourself and the space

Take note of the model for celebration at paragraphs 187-192, which can be used for each of the preparation rites. Read through the rites you intend to celebrate, underlining important passages and making notes for yourself.

Go to the space in which you will celebrate the rites. If you are not going to be in the church, decide what you will need to do to make the room you have chosen into a worship space. Is there a cross? Will you need a lectern? White cloth? A candle? A Bible or lectionary?

EPHPHETHA RITE

In the RCIA, this rite is placed after the Recitation of the Creed. However, the introduction says that if both are celebrated, the ephphetha rite is celebrated immediately before the recitation itself (186 and 194).

Ephphetha is an Aramaic word that means "be opened." Jesus uses the word in Mark's gospel when he heals the deaf man with a speech impediment. The RCIA says the symbolism of this rite "impresses on the elect their need of grace in order that they may hear the word of God and profess it for their salvation" (197).

After the homily or instruction on the Word (190 or 198), the presider invites the elect to stand. The godparents might also stand with them, keeping a hand on their shoulders, as a sign of support. The presider touches the ears and lips of the elect and pronounces the text given at paragraph 199.

RECITATION OF THE CREED

If for some reason you were not able to celebrate the presentation of the Creed, you would not celebrate the recitation (see paragraph 186). If you celebrated the ephphetha rite, the elect would return the Creed to the community immediately after. There is no text given to invite them to do so, so you will need to write one or ask the presider to improvise one.

CHOOSING A BAPTISMAL NAME

In the United States, there is no giving of a baptismal name (see paragraph 33.4). So this rite is not likely to be celebrated. However, you might take the occasion to reflect on the baptismal significance of the given names of the elect (200). This might be especially important if the Christian significance of a particular name is not immediately evident. I did this one year when we had a candidate named Pebbles. We baptized her as Pebbles, and we continue to pray that one day there will be a new saint added to the official litany.

All of these rites might be celebrated together in a single liturgy. Or, if the elect are gathered together for several hours or more, you might celebrate each rite individually.

For an outline of a parish retreat day that celebrates the preparation rites (written by Miriam Malone, SNJM), see TeamRCIA.com.

14 Initiation

The third and final doorway in the journey of the elect is their initiation. Turn your RCIA to number 206, and you will see what you probably already know: *initiation* "is the celebration of the sacraments of baptism, confirmation, and Eucharist."

The focus of the celebration here is the initiation of the elect, and the most appropriate place for that celebration is the Easter Vigil (207). However, initiation can take place outside the Easter Vigil, as long as we take care to ensure the rite "has a markedly paschal character" (208).

That "markedly paschal character" is what we want to focus on in our preparation of this liturgy. What is it that makes the initiation of the elect at the Vigil *paschal*?

A simple way to think of this is to look at all the elements of the Easter Vigil that focus on the death and resurrection of Jesus—the paschal mystery. The ultimate expression of that mystery, of course, is the Eucharist itself. Keep your finger on that page you have open in the RCIA and flip over to paragraph 217. Here you'll find the entire point of the initiation process:

Finally, in the celebration of the Eucharist…
    the newly baptized
reach the culminating point in their Christian initiation.…
When in communion they receive
the body that was given for us
and the blood that was shed,
the neophytes are strengthened

in the gifts they have already received

and are given a foretaste of the eternal banquet. (emphasis added)

Our goal in shaping the ritual, then, is to make the welcome of the newly baptized to the Table of the Lord the culmination of all that takes place at the Vigil.

PLANNING THE RITE

Of course you will want to read through the entire Easter Vigil and rites of initiation with a highlighter, pen, and notepad handy. If you look at the outline of the rite, you will see it has five major components:

1. Light

2. Word

3. Baptism

4. Confirmation

5. Eucharist

The first two are not dealt with in the RCIA, so you will need to figure out what to do with the elect during these portions of the liturgy.

Service of Light

Ask yourself what is *paschal* about this part of the liturgy. The paschal nature is the drama of the light breaking apart the darkness, and the climax of this portion is the hymn to the Light of Christ—the Exsultet. The question to ask ourselves is, what is the best way to use the liturgy to teach the elect that Christ is, indeed, the light that conquers darkness.

Obviously, this will be best accomplished if you begin the liturgy in actual darkness. This is, in fact, a universal requirement. According to the sacramentary: "The entire celebration of the Easter Vigil takes place at night. It should not begin before nightfall."

The paschal nature of the service of light is also made tangible if the light actually lights up the night. This is going to require a large fire, probably outdoors. And so the sacramentary directs us: "A large fire is prepared in a suitable place outside the church."

Ideally, then, all our parishes would be lighting a bonfire in pitch darkness to begin the Easter Vigil. The elect with their godparents would be placed at the front of the assembly to witness the full effect of the darkness being consumed by the light.

If your parish has never had the paschal fire outside the church, walk around the parish grounds and figure out the best place to do so. Imagine where people will stand, how you will direct them to gather around the fire, and how you will get the paschal candle lit.

When will the individual candles in the assembly be lit? Outside to prepare for the procession into the church, or at the doors of the church itself? The rite does not say if the elect have lit candles at this point, but it seems best that they do not. They will receive their lit candles after baptism.

Decide how you will place the elect in procession into the church where they will hear the Exsultet and the proclamation of the word of God, and decide where they will sit when they enter the church.

Liturgy of the Word

The lectionary provides nine readings (seven from the Old Testament and two from the New Testament) for the Easter Vigil. The sacramentary tells us, "The number of readings from the Old Testament may be reduced for pastoral reasons, but it must always be borne in mind that the reading of the word of God is the fundamental element of the Easter Vigil."

That is a very powerful statement. Of all that goes on at the Vigil, the readings are *the* fundamental element. What's fundamental about them—more so than anything else?

It is, of course, that it was God's living word that first spoke to the hearts of the elect and called them to this moment. It was our willingness to embody God's word—to be Christ for them—that has sustained them on their long journey. Our most pastoral response at this moment is to be indulgent with the proclamation of the God's Word. This is no time for expediency and efficiency. Strive to proclaim all nine readings. If that isn't possible, reduce the number with great care, retaining those readings that speak most powerfully of the paschal mystery.

The sacramentary requires that at least three of the Old Testament readings be read and that of those, the reading of Exodus 14 must be included. Why Exodus 14? It is the story of the original Passover—the word from which we get *paschal*. Jesus recast the Passover story, passing over from death to life, just as the Israelites passed over the Red Sea from slavery to freedom.

CELEBRATION OF BAPTISM

The RCIA itself begins with the celebration of baptism, which takes place immediately after the homily. Read what paragraph 209 has to say about this part of the rite: "The celebration of baptism has as its center and high point the baptismal washing and the invocation of the Holy Trinity."

So ask yourself, what is markedly *paschal* about the baptismal washing? There are many associate rites here, which are noted in the same paragraph: the blessing of water, the renunciation of sin, the profession of faith, the clothing with white garments, and the presentation of candles. With all this complicated activity, what will you do to make the baptism itself stand out as the high point? What will you do to make it markedly paschal?

Okay, to see what the RCIA expects, you're going to need to do some flipping around. First look at paragraph 213.

Therefore in the celebration of baptism
the washing with water
should take on its full importance
as the sign of that mystical sharing
in Christ's death and resurrection
through which those who believe in his name
die to sin and rise to eternal life. (emphasis added)

There's that paschal emphasis. The rite expects that however we do the baptisms, they seem fully important. They should seem so important that each baptism says something about Christ's death and resurrection and the candidates' death to sin and resurrection in new life.

The paragraph goes on to suggest that this could be done either by immersion or the pouring of water, but that however it's done, it does not seem to be "a mere purification rite."

Now keep in mind that this part of the RCIA is written for the universal church. Different cultures around the world may interpret immersion and pouring somewhat differently. When the bishops in the United States read that paragraph, they wanted to exercise their teaching authority to explain how baptism in the U.S. would best give a sense of dying and rising.

To see that, you have to turn to Appendix III in the RCIA, "National Statutes for the Catechumenate":

Baptism by immersion is the fuller and more expressive sign of the sacrament and, therefore, is preferred. (17)

So there you have it. In order to make the baptism itself the high point of this part of the liturgy and to make it clearly prominent in relation to all the smaller associated rites, you will want to prepare for baptism by full immersion. If your parish does not have a full immersion font, you'll want to be in touch with the carpenters and plumbers in your parish to assist you in creating a temporary font for the Vigil.

Now flip back to the ritual itself and walk through each portion of the rite. Pay attention to rubrics, underline important points, and make notes for yourself. Here are a few things to keep in mind.

Presentation of the candidates

The celebration of baptism begins after the homily. See paragraphs 218-219. The RCIA provides three options, and you need to choose based on where your baptismal font is located. Note that in each option, the rite places great emphasis on the assembly being able to see the baptisms. And in each option, the candidates are called by name. It adds to the solemnity of the rite if their names are chanted instead of merely spoken. If you choose to do that, make a note to yourself to speak with the musicians about it.

Once their names are called (or chanted) their godparents bring the candidates to the font. Depending on where the font is located, the assembly might also be called to gather around or face the font. If there is a procession of the entire assembly to the font, option B at paragraph 219 gives the order of the procession. The litany of saints is sung during the procession.

Invitation to prayer

Note the permission for adaptation in the rubrics (220).

Litany of saints

The rubrics allow for the addition of other saint names in the litany. If the names of the candidates are not already among the names listed, ask the musicians to add them (see paragraph 221). There is a bit of a gray area if the given name of the candidate is not a saint's name. I think that the year we baptized Pebbles, the musician may have slipped her name in there. If you want to keep the actual litany to the traditional saints, note the end of the litany that reads: "Give new life to these chosen ones by the grace of baptism." At that point the cantor might sing the names of the chosen ones—that is, the candidates for baptism.

Prayer over the water

There are three options listed here (222), but option A is the only one used at the Vigil itself. This blessing is ideally sung, so make a note to have the presider practice with the musicians ahead of time.

Profession of faith

The profession of faith (223) is a two-part process: the renunciation of sin (224), followed by the actual profession (225). The renunciation may be done individually or as a group. Keep in mind the number of elect you will have at the Vigil and imagine how either option will sound. The profession of faith is made by each candidate individually, immediately before baptism. If you are doing full immersion baptisms, the profession might be made once the candidate is actually in the water.

Baptism

The rubrics suggest a sung acclamation after each baptism (226), so make a note to speak with the musicians. Also pay attention to the rubric that allows for the candidates to be divided into groups if you have a large number of baptisms.

You will also want to consider what the candidates wear for the baptism. Whether you are doing immersion or pouring, both assume the candidates are thoroughly drenched. Make a note to have the godparents alert them. They don't want to be wearing their finest clothes. Some parishes advise the candidates to dress in lightweight cotton clothes that won't absorb as much water as denim or wool. Other parishes provide a brown or gray robe for the candidates to wear.

During the baptism itself, the godparents need to be in physical contact with their candidates. Walk around the font, and imagine where everyone is placed— the godparents, the candidate, the presider. Also think about what happens to the neophytes immediately after they are baptized. If you are doing full immersion, you're going to need towels. Where will they be stored? Who will bring them to the dripping neophytes? Will the neophytes depart immediately to change or remain to witness the other baptisms?

While the neophytes are changing into their dry clothes, the assembly will be singing. Be sure the musicians have planned sufficient music.

Explanatory rites

ANOINTING AFTER BAPTISM

The anointing after baptism would not be done. Read the rubric at paragraph 228 that says this only takes place if confirmation is not going to immediately follow. Confirmation will always take place in conjunction with baptism at the Easter Vigil. To see why, flip back to paragraph 215:

In accord with the ancient practice
    followed in the Roman liturgy,
adults are not to be baptized
without receiving confirmation immediately afterward....
The conjunction of the two celebrations
    signifies the unity of the paschal mystery,
    the close link between the mission of the Son
    and the outpouring of the Holy Spirit....

The term "adults" in the RCIA refers to anyone who has reached catechetical age, that is, about the age of seven. So if you have elect who are children, they would be confirmed at the Vigil even if diocesan policy has set an older age for the confirmation of previously baptized children. See paragraphs 252 and 305 and also National Statutes for the Catechumenate, 18.

CLOTHING WITH A BAPTISMAL GARMENT

The clothing with a white garment is optional (229), but is done in almost every parish. The smoothest way to do this is to have the candidates don their white garments when they are changing out of their wet clothes after baptism. The rite, however, envisions the godparents placing the garment on their neophytes within the ritual itself. Imagine how it will work best in your community.

Also be sure to plan for having enough garments on hand. Will you have parishioners make them, or do you plan to purchase them?

You also want to consider how the neophytes return to the assembly. Will they simply re-enter the worship space, one by one, as they are ready? Or will they return all together?

PRESENTATION OF A LIGHTED CANDLE

The final element in the baptismal ritual is the giving of the candle (230). The godparents light the neophytes' candles from the Easter candle and present it to the newly baptized.

Now if you leave it to the godparents to acquire these candles ahead of time, they are most likely to purchase one of those anemic looking tapers sold in Catholic supply houses across the country. Invest some time and money to find substantial, quality candles that can be used for years on the anniversary of baptism at family meals.

CELEBRATION OF CONFIRMATION

Walk around your worship space and imagine the best place for celebrating the confirmation (231) of the newly baptized. Will it be at the font or in the sanctuary? Which spot allows for the fullest participation of the assembly? Don't forget that the godparents will be standing with them and should keep a hand on their shoulders at all times.

Notice that the rubric reiterates the authority of a priest who baptizes to also confirm (232). He does not need any additional authorization from the bishop. Notice also that other ministers of confirmation may assist if there are a great number of candidates.

Invitation

The RCIA gives permission to adapt the invitation (233). The example text in the book might benefit from shortening.

Laying on of hands

The rite directs the minister of confirmation to stretch out his hands over all the candidates for confirmation (234). If there are not too many candidates, the symbol is much more powerful if the presider lays hands individually on each one. Pretend to do this yourself, checking the pacing and the location of the candidates. If there isn't enough room to lay hands comfortably, perhaps you want to rethink the location where you will have them stand.

Anointing with chrism

Go through the same imaginary process with the anointing. Notice that the ritual directs the minister to dip his thumb in the chrism and make the sign of the cross (235). However, the symbol will create a more powerful and deeper memory if he pours the oil onto the head of the candidate and uses his whole hand to make the sign of the cross. After they are anointed, they exchange a sign of peace with the presider, and their godparents return with them to their places in the assembly.

Renewal of baptismal promises

At this point, the assembly would stand with lighted candles and renew their baptismal promises. Following that, they would be sprinkled with the blessed baptismal water. (See RCIA 237-240.)

LITURGY OF THE EUCHARIST

The RCIA says very little about the Liturgy of the Eucharist even though it is the culmination of the entire journey of the new initiates. Here is a possible way to structure the rite to emphasize the paschal nature of this moment.

Note that paragraph 243 indicates the presider might briefly remind the neophytes of the preeminence of the Eucharist, "which is the climax of their initiation and the center of the whole Christian life." This exhortation takes place after the sign of peace, immediately after the Lamb of God. The power of the exhortation will have a stronger effect if the presider or another minister first calls the newly baptized by name.

At the calling of each name, the godparents walk the neophytes to a place nearer the altar (but not *at* the altar). The godparents stay with their neophytes with their hands on their shoulders.

Then the presider speaks directly to the newly baptized. All that is needed is a sentence or two, perhaps based on a psalm, that calls attention to the moment. Here's an example:

> My dear friends, come—taste and see the goodness of the Lord. You and we have longed for this moment for so many months [and years]. Behold, this is the Lamb of God….

After taking Communion himself, the presider calls the newly baptized to come forward to the altar to share in Communion. Then, before the rest of the community, the newly baptized partake of the body and blood of Christ for the first time. The musicians might lead the assembly in an alleluia or other acclamation of praise after each neophyte receives Communion. Or they might begin the Communion processional song.

Think about when the godparents will share in Communion. If it can be done conveniently, the best option might be to have them accompany the neophytes to their seats in the assembly and then join the usual Communion procession. In that way, the ritual gives greater emphasis to the "first" Communions.

The neophytes would then return to their places in the assembly, and the rest of the liturgy would proceed as normal.

PART FOUR

NUTS AND BOLTS

15

How to Build Your Team

W ow, all this sounds like a lot of work, doesn't it? How in the world are you going to manage it all? The first thing to realize is, especially if you are in a small parish, much of the "work" of the catechumenate is the ordinary work of parish life. Catechumens learn to be Catholic by hanging out with other Catholics. Since that's the case, the most important team member you have is the parish community.

THE FAITHFUL

Let me say it again. The most important member of your team already exists. You are not creating anything new. You are enhancing and building on what's already there. Get your RCIA book and turn to paragraph 9. Underline this phrase, about three lines down: "the initiation of adults is the responsibility of all the baptized."

Now repeat this mantra: "Initiation is not my job. It's their job." *Your* job is to help the parishioners do their job. The RCIA gives you a five-point outline of the job description for the faithful—the parishioners: evangelization, liturgy, election Sunday, Lent, and Easter. Let's take a look at it together (still in paragraph 9).

1. Evangelization

"[T]the faithful should remember that…the supreme purpose of the apostolate is that Christ's message is made known to the world by word and deed and that his grace is communicated."

How in the world are they going to do that? Like this (9.1):

1. Live like a Christian *in a way the catechumens can see them doing so*
2. Invite the catechumens into their homes
3. Talk to the catechumens
4. Invite the catechumens to community gatherings

That's what *they* have to do. What *you* have to do is think up creative ways to help the [parishioners do these things. Don't fall into the rut of taking on these tasks yourself. Sit down right now, and list twenty ways you can encourage the parishioners to take on their role. I started a list on TeamRCIA.com. You can go there to see mine and add your own twenty.

2. Liturgies

Whenever you celebrate a ritual with the catechumens, "the faithful should seek to be present…and should take an active part in the responses, prayers, singing, and acclamations" (9.2).

Can you think of twenty ways to help them do that? Come up with your own list before you check out mine.

3. Election Sunday

The election of the catechumens is a *huge* event. It really ought to be second only to the Easter Vigil in your parish. It is like a couple that has been dating for a long time finally announcing their engagement. Like an engagement, the election of the catechumens doesn't just change them; it changes the entire parish family.

"On the day of election, because it is a day of growth for the community, the faithful, when called upon, should be sure to give honest and carefully considered testimony about the catechumens" (9.3).

Obviously, if the faithful have not been involved in the lives of the catechumens during the inquiry and catechumenate stages, they won't be able to give honest testimony. So points one and two are critical in helping the parishioners fulfill the third point of their job description. Assuming you've gotten them this far, what are twenty things you can do to help them testify? Once you have your list, check out mine at TeamRCIA.com.

4. Lent

"[T]he faithful should take care to participate in the rites of the scrutinies and presentations and give the elect the example of their own renewal....At the Easter Vigil, they should attach great importance to renewing their own baptismal promises." (9.4)

Give me twenty, and then check mine at TeamRCIA.com.

5. Easter

"[T]he faithful should take part in the Masses for neophytes..., welcome the neophytes with open arms in charity, and help them to feel more at home in the community of the baptized." (9.5)

Got your twenty? If you do, compare them to mine.

TEAM LEADER

This person has the overall responsibility for the catechumenate. In the RCIA text, the job description for the team leader is described in terms of the duties of the pastor. The pastor is an essential member of the team, and he does have the overall responsibility for the catechumenate. However, as with many of his other responsibilities, much of his role as catechumenate team leader can be delegated. We're going to assume that's the case in your parish and assume the team leader is someone other than the pastor.

The team leader might also be called the catechumenate coordinator or the director of the catechumenate. If you open your rite book to paragraph 13 and substitute "team leader" for "priests," you'll get a pretty good overview of what the leader's role is:

- Attending to the pastoral care of the catechumens
- Providing instruction
- Approving the choice of godparents
- Planning and coordinating the celebration of the rites

That is a broad and general job description that needs to be fleshed out for your specific situation. If you are reading this book because your pastor has designated you as the team leader, and if you are just starting out, the discrete tasks can begin to look overwhelming. Take a big breath. Like the pastor, it is not your job to *do* all these things. It is your job to *see that they get done*.

If you are reading this book because you are trying to decide who should be the team leader, find someone who is good at seeing the big picture and who can delegate well. More specifically, here is a short list of characteristics of a good team leader:

1. **Enthusiastic.** There are a lot of ups and downs in developing an initiation process. A good leader has to see the upside a lot more than the downside.

2. **Confident.** There is plenty of opportunity for second guessing and self-doubt in a fledgling initiation process. A team leader needs to be confident of her abilities and the abilities of the rest of the team. She needs to be able to instill confidence in them.

3. **Flexible.** Something will go wrong. Some days, everything will go wrong. Other days, things will be unclear, uncertain, or unscripted. A good leader is flexible enough to take whatever is "wrong" or unknown and turn it into a learning opportunity.

4. **Excellent.** Being flexible does not mean being lax. A good leader will strive for excellence in every aspect of the catechumenate process.

5. **Passionate.** The pastoral care of the inquirers and catechumens should be the number one driving force for the team leader.

6. **Prayerful.** A team leader understands that she is a servant. The discipline of regular prayer, both personal and liturgical, is what keeps her obedient to her call to service.

OTHER TEAM MEMBERS

If you are in a small parish, the team members might consist of the parish assembly, the pastor, and the team leader. If that's the case, much of the week-to-week work of the initiation process will fall to the team leader alone.

If you are in a medium-size parish, the team leader might wear another hat or two, but she will have two to six others who will assist in ongoing activities.

In large parishes, a team leader needs to focus on leading, coordinating, developing, and training key team members.

As we look at who some additional team members might be, keep in mind that depending on the size of your parish, the team leader might be doing double or triple (or more) duty to see that the process happens.

AMBASSADOR OF WELCOME (INQUIRY COORDINATOR)

If you are in a small parish and you can only find one other person to help, this is the person to find. In some parishes, this person might be called the inquiry coordinator or the precatechumenate coordinator. But those titles sound so sterile to me. The person in charge of inquiry is really someone who is constantly on the lookout for people who need more joy in their lives. He is especially on the lookout for those who are not yet deeply connected to the life of the parish. The folks that will be attracted to him are not necessarily people who are looking to "become Catholic." They are looking for something that is missing in their lives. They are looking to fill a hole or heal a wound.

A secondary role the ambassador of welcome might fill is to be an initial recruiter of more team members. Ideally, the ambassador of welcome is an extrovert who loves networking and meeting new people. He can be alert to those who might have gifts to offer the catechumenate process.

For those who are regular members of the parish, there are other ministries that help with their seeking or their grief. Their needs are fundamentally different from the needs of those who don't know Christ or don't fully understand their relationship with Christ. The ambassador of welcome is an evangelist who brings good news to those who have not heard it before. These are some of the qualities you will want to look for in an ambassador of welcome:

1. *Joyful.* Hard to be the ambassador of joy if you're not joyful. But the joy needs to flow from their love of Christ, not because they won the lotto.

2. *Story-hearer.* This person has to love to *listen* to stories. Other people's more than his own.

3. *Prayerful.* Beyond the role prayer plays in keeping us true to our ministry, this person will also be someone who can pray for the inquirers and who asks for and receives insight into what their individual needs are.

4. *Flexible.* But not exactly in the same way as the team leader. There is little that can go "wrong" in the inquiry period. What does often happen, however, is the inquirer is led to a path other than the catechumenate. An ambassador of welcome needs to be genuinely happy they are taking another step on their own journey and not be disappointed that he "lost one."

5. *Extroverted.* An ambassador of welcome loves to meet new people and thinks of every new person as an interesting story about to unfold.

CATECHIST

In a small parish, you might be the only catechist. Even so, keep your eyes open for someone who can assist you and perhaps even lead the catechetical sessions on occasion to give you a break.

To find a true catechist, or to develop the charism of a catechist within yourself, you have to sit down and have a conversation with yourself. What is it a catechist *does*?

Pope John Paul II said the primary aim of catechesis is to bring people into intimate communion with Jesus Christ. Our model for doing this is going to be the community of first disciples. How did they learn who Jesus was? How did they grow intimate with him? How do they help others, who have never met Jesus, become intimate with him? That original catechetical process looked a lot like hanging out and not so much like school.

> "The definitive aim of catechesis is to put people not only in touch but in communion, in intimacy, with Jesus Christ...."
>
> *Pope John Paul II,*
> *On Catechesis in Our Time, 5*

That doesn't mean Jesus didn't teach. But he taught by example, through storytelling, by developing a mentoring or apprenticing relationship, by dining, exhorting, correcting, and sacrificing.

A true catechist isn't someone who simply shows up in response to a call for volunteers. Many times, someone who has this gift doesn't think of herself as a "teacher." You'll need to pay attention to those in the parish you might be able to develop into this role.

For example, I know a real estate agent in a nearby parish. She has two Web sites that she updates regularly and has written a book on how to sell your house. If you spend more than 15 minutes talking with her, you'll also find out she has a small theology library in her home and two of her relatives are Jesuits. She is a lector in her parish, and she often disagrees with the way this or that word in the lectionary was translated from the original Greek. As far as I know, she has no teaching experience, and no one has ever asked her to be a catechist. If I were in her parish, I would.

There is another person I met several years ago in my parish. She is a nutritionist and, at the time, was a member of a group of adult Catholics who were preparing for confirmation. She argued with me a lot, not so much challenging my knowledge, but testing how much I believed what I said. She had no theological library and no Jesuits in her family. But she took her faith seriously and wanted to be sure those who were guiding her took theirs just as seriously. She turned out to be a fine catechist.

You know people like this. They don't fit a "mold," and they may not make your life very easy. But they are intelligent and creative and filled with faith. These are the kinds of people you want to recruit to be catechists.

If you are in a medium-size parish, you want to have at least four to five catechists on your team so no one gets overburdened. I prefer assigning a catechist for a liturgical season, rather than rotating every Sunday. That way the catechists can develop more of an ongoing relationship with the catechumens.

When you are looking for a catechist, here are some essential qualities:

1. **Faithful.** A catechist has to be a person of deep faith.

2. **Catholic.** I don't mean just someone who was baptized and goes to Mass. I mean someone *Catholic*, who loves being Catholic, who loves all the beauty and complexity of what it means to be Catholic. I *do not* mean this person is never disappointed or frustrated with the Catholic institution. But the disappointments pale next to the joy of living the Catholic life.

3. **Scriptural.** A catechist doesn't have to be a Scripture scholar, but she does need to know the central stories that are proclaimed throughout the liturgical year.

4. **Traditional.** This is not the same as "conservative" or "not-liberal." Those are political labels that are not helpful in the catechumenate. "Traditional" in this sense means the catechist knows and lives the tradition of the church. Again, masters-level theology is not required. But she needs to be up to speed on basic Catholic teaching.

5. **Curious.** A good catechist realizes she is not the answer-lady (or answer-guy). She is learning more about Jesus all the time, just as the catechumens are.

SPONSOR COORDINATOR

In a small parish, you are likely going to be the sponsor coordinator, perhaps with the assistance of an ambassador of welcome. In a medium to large parish, you will want to delegate that role to someone. You might even have a team of two or three people who share this role. A sponsor coordinator has three tasks:

1. Recruitment

2. Training

3. Support

Recruitment of sponsors will be an ongoing concern in most parishes. Catholics are not used to volunteering for the role of sponsor. And, while the tasks of being a sponsor are not difficult, there is a large time commitment. An effective sponsor coordinator is patient and persistent. She thinks ahead and starts planting seeds with potential sponsors who are too busy to serve now, but might be available next year or the year after.

An effective sponsor coordinator will have these qualities:

1. **Patient.** At times, she will need the patience of Job.

2. **Intuitive.** An effective sponsor coordinator will have an eye for hidden talent and a willingness to ask out-of-the-ordinary folks to serve.

3. **Persistent.** A good sponsor coordinator is a bit of a mother hen, constantly checking in, making sure the sponsors are doing their jobs. Also, she is a person who other people have trouble saying no to.

4. **Listens.** Sponsors are like all people. They will have frustrations and fears. The sponsor coordinator needs to be a good listener.

SPONSORS

Sponsors are chosen and assigned by the parish (that's you) and not by the catechumen. A catechumen has little idea what the qualifications of a sponsor are. The catechumen, once his formation is nearly complete, will choose a godparent, who might be the sponsor or might be someone different than his sponsor. However, by that time, the catechumen will have a clear idea of the responsibilities of a godparent and will be able to choose wisely.

Finding the right sponsor for the right candidate is a matchmaking process. You probably have some matchmaking skills because they parallel other ministry skills. If you don't think you would be a good matchmaker though—or if the size of your parish and team means you are already fully occupied—seek out someone to help you coordinate the sponsors and match them to the catechumens.

Some qualities of sponsors include:

1. **Faithful.** A sponsor is a person of faith and a practicing Catholic.

2. **Questioning.** The sponsor will learn a lot as she accompanies the catechumen. She shouldn't be afraid to ask questions about things she doesn't know about. Her willingness to ask is a good example to the catechumen.

3. **Hospitable.** A sponsor is always hospitable and charitable toward the catechumen. She remembers birthdays and family names.

4. **Disciplined.** A sponsor lives the life she expects the catechumen to live. And she holds both herself and the catechumen accountable for living that life.

Where to find sponsors

Sponsors usually come from one of three places. The most helpful for the sake of the catechumens and the team are parishioners the team has discerned to have the right gifts and have been recruited specifically for the role of sponsor.

Another source of sponsors is a general plea to the parish—in the bulletin, on the Web site, or during the announcements at Mass. A sponsor coordinator should persistently use these avenues, but not too many people will respond to a general plea. Think of how you got involved. Did you answer an ad in the bulletin, or did someone ask you directly?

The third is a person the inquirer brings and asks to have designated as sponsor. In most cases this sponsor is going to need a significant amount of training. It is also possible he or she is not far enough along on the conversion journey to completely fulfill the role of sponsor. You will have to discern how much support the sponsor is going to need in order to serve in this ministry. You might consider pairing this person with a second sponsor whom the team chooses. It might be a burden to your team, but think of it as another opportunity to invite someone deeper into the paschal mystery.

20 IDEAS FOR FINDING SPONSORS

To be a sponsor is to make a big commitment. Sometimes we undersell the commitment part, trying not to scare people away. All that does is say to the volunteer, "I'm not really going to ask very much of you because I don't think you'd really want to do this anyway." Believe it or not, there are many people in your parish who are looking to make a big commitment. Try to emphasize the important contribution the sponsor *must* make to the lives of the catechumens and how essential it is to the gospel mission that people like him make a sacrifice for the sake of the faith.

Also, ask the people who are likely to say yes. A sponsor is not someone sitting at home with nothing to do. *That* person has already said no a thousand times. That's why he has so much free time. Here's a list of 20 kinds of people to ask to be sponsors.

1. Those who have *completed* their neophyte year.
2. The spouses of the newly initiated (not spouses of the catechumens).
3. The parents of the newly initiated (not parents of the catechumens).
4. The in-laws of the newly initiated (not in-laws of the catechumens).
5. The president of the parish council, six months before his term expires.
6. A Catholic school teacher, six months before her retirement.

7. A retired priest.

8. A retired sister.

9. The chairperson of *last year's* banquet committee.

10. All the communion ministers.

11. All the lectors.

12. All the ushers.

13. The parish's top ten financial contributors.

14. All the single mothers who baptized a baby within the last five years.

15. All the grandparents of those babies.

16. All the ex-teenagers who were confirmed five years ago.

17. The parents of all the children who have celebrated first Communion within the last five years.

18. The grandparents of those children.

19. All the "Protestants married to Catholics" who were received into the Catholic Church in the last five years.

20. All of the choir members.

Duties of a sponsor

So what does a sponsor need to do? Every sponsor-companion relationship is unique, but, in general, a good analogy is a coach and athlete. Or drama coach and actor. Or music coach and musician. Like these other kinds of learners, the catechumens are learning a new way of living in the world. They are practicing a discipline. The coach isn't exactly a teacher. He is someone who knows how to play ball or play the piano. He watches and listens and offers guidance, encouragement, and maybe even rides the athlete, actor, or musician a little when they slack off.

This analogy implies sponsors have to be more expert than they are. What sponsors have to be expert at is living like Catholics. They don't have to be saints or theologians, but they should be churchgoing, active members of the parish. Their family and work lives should reflect their Catholic values.

In small parishes, that describes a large chunk of the parish. In medium-size parishes, between you, the parish staff, and the parish council, you should be able to easily name at least 200 people who fit that description. In large parishes, it will be impossible to know all the potential sponsors, and it can be an exciting adventure trying to discover who they might be.

DISMISSAL MINISTERS

This is a made-up role. The RCIA says the catechumens are dismissed from Mass before the Creed and the prayer of the faithful, but it says nothing about what they do after they are dismissed. Because most parishes don't want to simply send the catechumens away, they send a minister out with them to lead them in a breaking open the word session.

You or your catechists might serve as dismissal ministers. However, this is an excellent opportunity to involve more of the parish. Anyone who has participated in a RENEW group, a TEC or Cursillo retreat, a small Christian community, or has simply shared faith over Scripture can lead a dismissal session. This isn't formal catechesis. It is faith sharing. It is more like prayer than Bible study. You could ask parishioners to sign up for a single Sunday a month or even a Sunday a quarter to lead the catechumens in faith sharing over the Sunday readings and the homily. Once the catechumens become skilled in the process, they could even lead the faith sharing themselves.

The qualities of a dismissal minister include:

1. **Faithful.** A good dismissal minister has an active faith life that is enlivened by the word proclaimed at Mass. And he is willing to share that faith with others.

2. **Talkative.** If you have a new group of catechumens, chances are they won't share too much or too deeply at first. It helps to have someone who can lead the conversation along.

3. **Generous.** While you want someone who can keep the conversation going, you don't want a person who needs all the attention in the room. At the first inkling of input from a catechumen, the dismissal minister needs to allow some space for the catechumen to respond.

PASTOR AND CLERGY

As we mentioned, the pastor has the overall responsibility for the initiation process in the parish. However, he usually delegates a great deal of that to the team leader. The team leader *might be* another member of the ordained—an associate pastor or a deacon. Designating a team leader is a discernment process, and pastors will want to struggle with this for a while to make the best decision for the parish. Ordination, by itself, does not necessarily qualify someone to lead the catechumenate team.

On the other hand, presiding and preaching at the rites are roles that are specifically designated for the ordained. The pastor will want to be sure the clergy in the parish are learning the rites and spending time rehearsing them. The pastor needs to see to it that the homilists of the parish are crafting their preaching for the rites and for the presence of the catechumens in the Sunday assembly each week.

The deacon's role is more flexible. There are rites at which only they or a priest may preside. There are other rites and prayers at which either they or a lay person may preside. A deacon may also serve in any of the other team roles, and he should spend some time discerning with the pastor and the team leader where his gifts can best serve the community. The pastor and the team leader should also keep in mind that, if the deacon is married, his wife usually has the same level of training as her husband and can also be an effective minister in a team role.

OTHER MINISTERS

There are many other things that need to be done to sustain your catechumenate. If you are in a large parish, you might have folks specifically on your team dedicated to these tasks. However, in most parishes, you will draw upon the talents of the folks who are already doing these ministries in the parish.

LITURGY AND PRAYER LEADERS

Somebody in your parish is good at understanding how ritual works. If you're lucky, you already know who that is. Maybe it's you! But if you don't know who it is, you will need to do a little detective work. You are not necessarily looking for a trained liturgist (but if you have one in your parish, by all means, start there!). You are looking for someone who has a sense of drama and who understands how symbols work. It could be a musician, someone trained in dance, someone with an acting background, or someone on the art and environment committee who is always fussing to make sure things are just so.

One of the best "liturgists" I ever knew was a soccer mom. She had three young children—all over-involved in sports and music—and a busy husband. Her goal was to make their home a place of beauty and harmony, even in the midst of chaos. She was a *natural* when it came to planning and coordinating the Easter Vigil.

Also, keep in mind this isn't necessarily one person. It might be the liturgy committee. Or one person might be better at leading a rehearsal and another person at leading small group prayer. Be creative, and think of ways to draw more people into your team.

HOSPITALITY

Every parish I know of has a kitchen crew, a lunch lady, a baker, or someone who just likes to put on coffee and set out some cookies. They may not think of themselves as catechumenate team members, but they are essential to you. If there are enough of these folks in your parish, see if they would be willing to provide coffee and snacks for your weekly catechetical sessions. At a minimum, you will need receptions for the candidates and parishioners after the Easter Vigil, the Rite of Sending, and the Rite of Acceptance.

Beyond providing food, ask a few folks in the parish if they would go out of their way to chat with the catechumens each week. Catholics can be shy, but if they feel like they have a job to do, they will usually follow through. Make it somebody's job to reach out to the catechumens.

RETREAT LEADERS

You and your catechists are likely going to be the ones who design and lead the retreats for the catechumens. However, here are some ideas for adding retreat leaders to your team. If your parish has a youth minister, see if she might help you with retreats. Or check with the youth minister at a nearby parish. If you live in an urban area, consider joining with other parishes to provide deanery or regional retreats for the catechumens. Oftentimes, folks on the diocesan staff are experienced retreat leaders. Some of them may have moved into administration and might enjoy being back in the field. The same is true for some professors at Catholic colleges—even if they teach in the math department.

PRAY-ERS

This is so easy and obvious it sometimes gets overlooked. Make lists of every parish group you can think of, and rotate through them asking them to pray for specific catechumens at specific moments in their journey. Don't overlook the elderly and the homebound. Avoid general appeals. Putting a notice in the bulletin asking everyone to pray for the catechumens doesn't make anyone feel like part of the team. But if you ask the women's guild members to each take the name of someone about to celebrate the Rite of Acceptance, and pray for that person for nine days (a novena), you will have significantly added to your team.

16 The Itinerary: A Step-by-Step Guide for Starting the RCIA in Your Parish

A re you ready to get started on the journey? Where should you start? Sometimes just taking the first step is the most difficult part. Keep this in mind. It's not all up to you. You've come this far because you've been led by the Holy Spirit. You'll know what to do next and when to do it when the Spirit leads you. At the same time, I have a friend who says the Holy Spirit is not an excuse for not studying for the exam. You have to do your homework and prepare yourself as best you can. What follows is a week by week outline of *possible* steps you might take to get a team started. In the outline below, a "week" might be two or three weeks or a month in your parish. Adjust the timelines as needed for your situation.

And don't worry about going slow. Take things step by step, a day at a time. The reign of God is everlasting. You've got plenty of time.

WEEK 1

Perhaps you know who you want on your team, and perhaps you don't. Before you even start, you know the assembly is a huge part of your team. The pastor is also a key team member. And there is you. If you have no one else in mind right now, that's fine. Schedule a meeting with the pastor for some brainstorming about who else in the parish might help out.

If you are in a small parish, you might be covering multiple roles and relying on others in the parish to help out occasionally. If you are in a medium or large size parish, try to come up with names of people who can fill these team roles:

1. Ambassador of Welcome (Inquiry coordinator)

2. Catechist(s). You will eventually want several, but you only need to find one to start.

3. Sponsor coordinator. You may not need to find this person in the first week, but keep thinking of who could do the job.

4. Count the pastor in

5. And yourself

During your meeting with the pastor, get your calendars out and schedule your meetings for the coming year. The pastor does not necessarily need to be at the weekly catechetical sessions (but if he can be, that's great!). He should, however, be at the initial team formation sessions. That's what you want to get calendared with him.

TASKS FOR WEEK 1

❑ In consultation with the pastor, create a list of potential team members.

❑ Order copies of the *Rite of Christian Initiation of Adults* for each member of your team. If you don't know how many team members you will have yet, order at least four copies. You can order more later if you need to.

❑ Establish a date for a team meeting within the next two weeks. Choose a date the pastor can be present.

❑ Contact potential team members. Ask them for a one-year commitment to the team.

When you invite potential team members to sign up, you don't necessarily need to assign them a role before the first meeting. As you read through the RCIA together and they begin to understand the process, they may self-select into different roles than you had first imagined them in.

WEEK 2

In the time before your initial team meeting, read as much of the RCIA as you can. Make notes and write down your questions. At the very least, you will need to read the introduction, paragraphs 1-35. Ideally, the pastor would also read at least the introduction before your initial team meeting. (Don't confuse Christian Initiation: General Introduction with the introduction to the RCIA. The General Introduction comes first, and, while it is good to read, it is not what we are discussing here.)

TASKS FOR WEEK 2

❏ You and the pastor read at least paragraphs 1-35 of the RCIA.

❏ Make notes, and write down questions.

WEEK 3

Gather the team for your initial meeting. Allow ninety minutes. This meeting will be very important for setting the template of how to do catechesis. The church tells us that all formation should be modeled on the catechumenate:

> The model for all catechesis is the baptismal catechumenate....This catechumenal formation should inspire the other forms of catechesis in both their objectives and in their dynamism. (*General Directory for Catechesis*, 59)

Obviously your team members are not catechumens, and you wouldn't treat them like catechumens. But you do want to use the principles from the catechumenate for forming the team to be catechumenate ministers. (We'll discuss the principles of forming catechumens later in the book.) In the catechumenate, the first thing that happens is a sharing of faith. And so it should be in our formation of catechumenate ministers. We should begin by sharing our faith with one another, perhaps by breaking open the Sunday gospel together.

It is important that we understand that this is not "extra." It is the heart of formation. If it takes more time than scheduled, so be it. Make up time somewhere else, and always give priority to faith sharing.

You might be saying to yourself that just letting people talk about their personal experience is not really teaching anyone anything. There are two ways to look at that. The way that Jesus taught was always through stories, and the stories came from his life or the lives of the people he grew up with and lived with. He never used a text book or a lesson plan. As you read the gospel, you can see the progression of the faith of the disciples. Early in Jesus' ministry, they didn't understand much. By Pentecost, they were, as we are, "other Christs" (*Catechism of the Catholic Church*, 2782).

When you are forming the catechumens, their stories and life experiences may require more reflection and guidance on the church's experience—of which they are now a part. But their experience is still the first place to start. With the *team* formation, we know they are already "other Christs" or else you wouldn't have asked them to be on the team. Of course they are not perfect, but they are deeply faithful Christians. That deep faith is the source of teaching for the entire group.

So always remember the first principle: *all faith formation begins with a reflection on our faith.* With that in mind, here is a potential outline for your first team meeting.

> *20 min.* Breaking open the word and faith sharing using last Sunday's gospel.
>
> *25 min.* Read half of the introduction to the RCIA. Take turns reading each paragraph out loud and discussing.
>
> *10 min.* Break.
>
> *25 min.* Continue reading and discussing the second half of the introduction, paragraph by paragraph.
>
> *10 min.* Conclude the meeting.
>   1. Make a list of next actions.
>   2. Brainstorm names of other potential team members if necessary.
>   3. Assign reading for the team to do: *RCIA*, paragraphs 36-40.
>   4. Schedule your next meeting for sometime in the following week.
>   5. Brief closing prayer.

TASKS FOR WEEK 3

❏ Hold your initial team meeting (90 minutes).

❏ Act on the "next actions" list that you generate from the meeting.

❏ Contact more potential team members if necessary.

❏ Read paragraphs 36-40 of the RCIA.

If you are in a small parish and you and the pastor are the only team members, you still want to begin with faith sharing. If possible, try to find at least one other person to join you simply for the faith sharing, even if they will not be serving on the team. For example, the parish council president, your spouse, someone from the choir, etc.

WEEK 4

Now it is time to hold your second team meeting. If you have invited new people onto the team, be sure they are caught up with their reading before the meeting. At this meeting, you will want to brainstorm the first steps for welcoming inquirers. If you haven't already done so, you will also need to decide who will be the ambassador of welcome who will lead that process. Here is a suggested outline for the ninety-minute meeting:

> Keep in mind, our week-to-week template is merely a guideline. You may be proceeding a lot slower than this based on your parish situation.

20 min. Breaking open the word and faith sharing using last Sunday's gospel.

25 min. If the team has read RCIA, paragraphs 36-40, lead a discussion. If they have not read it, read it a paragraph at a time and discuss.

10 min. Break.

25 min. Brainstorm next steps for starting an inquiry process. Designate an ambassador of welcome. If no one present steps forward or has the necessary gifts, brainstorm possible people within the parish to approach.

Set a date for launching your inquiry process two weeks from now.

10 min. Conclude the meeting.
1. Make a list of next actions.
2. Assign reading for the team to do: RCIA, paragraphs 75-80.
3. Schedule your next meeting for sometime in the following week.
4. Brief closing prayer.

TASKS FOR WEEK 4

❏ Hold your second team meeting (90 minutes).

❏ Brainstorm what your inquiry process will look like.

❏ Designate an ambassador of welcome.

❏ Act on the "next actions" list that you generate from your team meeting.

❏ Contact more potential team members if necessary.

❏ Read paragraphs 75-80 of the RCIA.

WEEK 5

This week is focused on ongoing formation for the team. If folks are feeling a little anxious or rushed, it is a good time to slow down and review what you've talked about and decided so far. If everyone is feeling comfortable, it is a good time to take some next steps toward evangelizing potential seekers. Remember to allow some additional time for faith sharing if the group feels energized and engaged in that portion of the agenda.

Hold your third team meeting. Schedule ninety minutes for the meeting.

20 min. Breaking open the word and faith sharing using last Sunday's gospel.

25 min. If the team has read RCIA, paragraphs 75-80, begin a discussion. If they have not read it, read it a paragraph at a time and discuss. Pay particular attention to paragraph 75.

10 min. Break.

25 min. Continue discussing RCIA, paragraphs 75-80.

10 min. Conclude the meeting.
1. Make a list of next actions.
2. Assign reading for the team to do: RCIA, paragraphs 118-128.
3. Schedule your next meeting for sometime in the following week.
4. Brief closing prayer.

TASKS FOR WEEK 5

❏ Hold your third team meeting (90 minutes).

❏ Act on the "next actions" list that you generate from the meeting.

❏ Amplify your evangelization efforts.

❏ Read paragraphs 118-128 of the RCIA.

What if you get an inquirer before you are "ready"? The Holy Spirit does not operate on your timeline. Someone may be knocking on your door right now, and the house is a mess. Instead of being anxious, be thankful that your parish is already attracting seekers. If you don't have a spot ready for the seeker yet, just have someone meet her for coffee or dessert. Keep in touch by phone and e-mail. All you really need to do right now is find out what her questions are. Let her know you will be learning together the best way to explore her questions. For more ideas, see Appendix 2.

WEEK 6

Week 6 is when things start in earnest. Whenever your "week 6" happens, you need to have a start date scheduled, and everyone needs to know when it is. If you aren't ready yet, delay it until it feels right. This is the date you formally start seeking seekers. Place announcements in the bulletin, local newspaper, Starbucks bulletin board, and anywhere else you can think of.

Make sure everyone inside the parish knows the start date and knows what to do when inquirers respond. The parish receptionist and anyone whose phone number or e-mail address is published in the bulletin or on the Web site should know how to respond to an inquirer. Everyone should know who the ambassador of welcome is and how to put the inquirer in touch with her. This is important. The receptionist, or whoever has been called, should get the name, phone number, and e-mail of the caller. Then the receptionist would contact the ambassador of welcome and give her the information. The ambassador of welcome would then return the inquirer's call. Ideally, this would all happen within the hour. It should absolutely happen within 24 hours.

Think of this call in a way similar to the way we think of a sick call. Every parish has a system for responding quickly to someone who calls for an emergency anointing or Communion for the dying. While you might not want to put the parish in that high of an alert for an inquiry call, you should be at least a "Level Orange." The primary mission of the parish is to evangelize. When someone calls us, essentially asking to be evangelized, we should drop everything else and attend to him.

So "Week 6" is your formal launch for your evangelization and inquiry process. It is also when you want to start thinking about sponsors. Once the inquirers start arriving, they will eventually need sponsors. If you haven't already done so, designate a sponsor coordinator.

Your fourth team formation session might look like this:

20 min. Breaking open the word and faith sharing using last Sunday's gospel.

25 min. If the team has read RCIA, paragraphs 118-128, begin a discussion. If they have not read it, read it a paragraph at a time and discuss.

10 min. Break.

10 min. Assess the launch of the evangelization and inquiry process. What has been done? What still needs to be done? What has worked well? What needs attention? What can you do to let more potential inquirers know about your parish?

15 min. If you haven't already done so, designate a sponsor coordinator. If no one present steps forward or has the necessary gifts, brainstorm possible people within the parish to approach. Set a date for implementing a sponsor recruitment program within the next two weeks. Set a date for a sponsor retreat and training day within the next month. If necessary, contact a retreat leader who can assist you in training the sponsors.

10 min. Conclude the meeting.

1. Make a list of next actions.
2. Assign reading for the team to do: RCIA, paragraphs 206-217 and 244-251.
3. Schedule your next meeting for sometime in the following week.
4. Brief closing prayer.

TASKS FOR WEEK 6

❏ Launch your evangelization and inquiry process.

❏ Hold your fourth team meeting (90 minutes).

❏ Assess the launch of your evangelization and inquiry process.

❏ Brainstorm what your sponsor recruitment process will look like.

❏ Designate a sponsor coordinator.

❏ Act on the "next actions" list that you generate from your team meeting.

❏ Read paragraphs 206-217 and 244-251 of the RCIA.

WEEK 7

Week 7 is the final intensive formation session for the team. You will want to have ongoing formation for them, of course, but by now they have a basic overview and understanding of how the RCIA works. You and the catechist(s) may want to continue to meet weekly for breaking open the word and faith sharing. Your other team members' growing commitments may keep them too busy to also continue meeting weekly. You should also be ready to meet with any of the team members individually to assist them with their roles, provide support, and offer more in-depth training.

Use Week 7 to assess how you are doing so far. Here is a possible outline:

20 min. Breaking open the word and faith sharing using last Sunday's gospel.

25 min. If the team has read RCIA, paragraphs 206-217 and 244-251, begin a discussion. If they have not read it, read it a paragraph at a time and discuss.

10 min. Break.

10 min. Continue to assess the evangelization and inquiry process. What has worked well? What needs attention? What can you do to let more potential inquirers know about your parish?

15 min. Assess the preparations for launching the sponsor recruitment program. What is on schedule? What needs attention?

10 min. Conclude the meeting.
1. Make a list of next actions.
2. If necessary, schedule another meeting for sometime in the following week.
3. Brief closing prayer.

TASKS FOR WEEK 7

❏ Continue to assess the launch of your evangelization and inquiry process.

❏ Assess the preparations for launching your sponsor recruitment process.

❏ Act on your "next actions" list.

17 Learning a Foreign Language: Catechesis

B rothers and sisters, we need to have a meeting and get it right about what we mean when we say "catechesis." We need to go into our mental memory banks and erase any neural connectors between "catechesis" and terms like "CCD," "religious education," "classes," and "programs." The *General Directory for Catechesis* puts it plainly:

> Catechesis is nothing other than the process of transmitting the Gospel, as the Christian community has received it, understands it, celebrates it, lives it, and communicates it in many ways. (105)

That cannot be reduced to a textbook or a series of classes. While catechesis is a "systematic" process of transmitting the Gospel, the system we use in the catechumenate is not a scope and sequence method drawn from secular pedagogy. The system we use is the celebration of the liturgical year, centered on the Easter Vigil.

The *General Directory for Catechesis* also says that the comprehensive and systematic nature of catechesis

> includes more than instruction: it is an apprenticeship of the entire Christian life, it is a "complete Christian initiation" [CT 21], which promotes an authentic following of Christ, focused on his Person.... (67)

The RCIA echoes this apprenticeship model of catechesis in paragraph 75:

> The catechumenate is an extended period during which the candidates are given suitable pastoral formation and guidance, aimed at training them in the Christian life.

As we discussed in chapter 5 on the catechumenate stage, this apprenticeship or training in the Christian life will take place in four broad categories: word, community, worship, and service.

WORD

Paragraph 75.1 of the RCIA says the catechumens are to receive a "suitable catechesis" in the dogmas of the church and the mystery of salvation.

The dogmas of the church and the revelation of the mystery of salvation flow from two sources: Scripture and tradition. The requirements for this "suitable catechesis" are also listed in paragraph 75.1. It is a catechesis that is to be:

1. gradual
2. complete
3. accommodated to the liturgical year
4. solidly supported by celebrations of the word

What that looks like practically is, once they have celebrated the Rite of Acceptance, the catechumens celebrate the Liturgy of the Word with us every Sunday. In the course of the liturgical year, "the entire mystery of Christ" is gradually unfolded (cf. General Norms for the Liturgical Year and the Calendar, 1). Following each weekly celebration of God's word, the catechumens participate in a process of exploring the mystery of Christ more deeply through Scripture and learning the tradition of the church. (See Appendix 4 for outlines of a dismissal and a catechetical session.)

COMMUNITY

Paragraph 75.2 calls upon the entire community to provide example and support for the catechumens in living the Christian life. Just as our metaphorical turnip heads learned by example, so do the catechumens. These are the things catechumens are to learn by living among other Christians:

1. how to turn to God in prayer
2. how to bear witness to the faith
3. how to believe in miracles and always feel hopeful
4. how to love their neighbors even if it means self sacrifice

That is a job description for a parish. The more parishioners live this kind of lifestyle, the more catechumens will learn how to live as Christians.

WORSHIP

Paragraph 75.3 of the RCIA tells us, "The Church, like a mother, helps the catechumens on their journey by means of suitable liturgical rites…." These rites will be primarily the Liturgy of the Word throughout the Sundays of the liturgical year. The catechumens will also celebrate other celebrations of the word and blessings in the context of their catechetical sessions. These liturgical celebrations are an integral part of living the Christian life and need to be understood as "catechetical." The quality of the liturgical celebration is formative. Good liturgy will form the catechumens well. Poor liturgy will form them badly.

SERVICE

Evangelization is a circular process. At some point in their lives, someone came to the catechumens with good news. Likewise, they should learn how to

1. spread the gospel
2. build up the church (75.4)

They learn how to do these things by becoming apprentices in the ministry of witness and the skill of professing their faith. Their witness and profession may be through acts of charity or words of consolation and hope. Whatever form their apostolic service takes, it is an essential part of their catechesis.

WHAT'S NEW?

This is a new way to think about catechesis for some of us. In the past, it was too easy to equate catechesis with textbook-style education. Today, our catechetical methods are going to need to be deeper than that. In order to bring people into a deep intimacy with Christ, our catechesis needs to begin with the experience of faith—both ours and the catechumen's.

In a previous era, we focused more on a mastery of intellectual knowledge, usually memorization of doctrines in question and answer format. We have grown to understand that the journey of faith is one of ongoing discernment in the four areas of catechesis described above. We do indeed discern the catechumens' mastery of doctrine, but that discernment is based on how the faith is lived out in word, community, worship, and service as much as on what the catechumens "know."

In the past, there was one path, one methodology, one timeline. We know that isn't how people really are. Now we understand that one size does not fit all.

Each catechumen will require a separate set of methods. And each will progress at a different rate.

What is new for some of us, and often difficult to understand, is that this complex and in-depth catechesis cannot be accomplished within the brief time-frame many parishes are accustomed to. The RCIA says,

> The duration of the catechumenate
>   will depend on the grace of God
>   and on various circumstances,
> such as
>   the program of instruction for the catechumenate,
>   the number of catechists, deacons, and priests,
>   the cooperation of the individual catechumens,
>   the means necessary
>   for them to come to the site of the catechumenate
>   and spend time there,
>   the help of the local community. (76)

The question every inquirer wants to know is, how long will this take? We don't want to seem harsh, and we certainly don't want them to go away, so we indicate that they will probably be baptized at the next Easter Vigil. While this seems like a pastoral response, it really isn't.

If you wanted to learn piano, how long would it take? If you wanted to fall in love, get engaged, get married, how long would it take? We cannot know such things at the beginning of the journey. It takes as long as it takes. And sometimes, it doesn't happen.

The RCIA goes on to say:

> Nothing, therefore, can be settled a priori.
> The time spent in the catechumenate
>   should be long enough—
>   several years if necessary—
>   for the conversion and faith of the catechumens
>   to become strong.
> By their formation
>   in the entire Christian life
>   and a sufficiently prolonged probation

the catechumens are properly initiated

    into the mysteries of salvation

    and the practice of an evangelical way of life. (76)

If the catechumens' faith has not become strong, if their formation has not prepared them for the rigors of the Christian life, if they are not well acquainted with the practices of an evangelical lifestyle, we are doing them no pastoral favors by initiating them before they are ready.

Will they be upset if you don't give them a firm date for baptism? Probably. Will they go to a neighboring parish that *will* give them a date? Or worse, will they leave altogether? Perhaps. But one thing is for sure. If we lead others on the way of the Cross without having done everything we can to prepare them, they will likely fall away even if they are already baptized.

THE FORMS OF CATECHESIS

The goal of catechesis is to bring catechumens to the point at which they are thinking, acting, talking, and walking like Christians. If you think of all the ways we form children to be functioning adults, you'll begin to see some of the possibilities for the many forms catechesis can take. In general, starting a successful catechetical process will look like this:

- Think up as many ways as possible to immerse the catechumens in the Catholic lifestyle

- Think up as many ways as possible to get them to reflect on their immersion experience

- Assess their reflections, and continue immersing them until they "get it"

Some of us who are more comfortable with a textbook model worry that a process like this won't be comprehensive enough. How do we know they learned everything? When do we teach them the doctrine?

Relax. I'm going to show you a way to make sure they learn everything and all the doctrine is covered. But in return, you have to be willing to let go of classroom models for assessing what they know. There are many ways to learn what people think and believe. Lecturing them and asking them to recite back what you lectured is only one way. And not a very effective one if your goal is intimacy with Christ.

SEE, DO, DISCUSS, REPEAT

When I got my first job in publishing, I had to master a complicated page-layout software program. My mentor did not lecture and did not give me a book to read. This is what she did:

1. She sat at my desk in front of the computer.

2. She performed a task while I looked over her shoulder.

3. We switched places, and I performed the task.

4. We compared her results to my results and discussed why I thought hers looked better.

5. I tried again, with new information from our discussion.

The process went on like that until I got comfortable enough to try things on my own, without her looking over my shoulder. I'd bring her the results of my work, and we'd discuss ways to improve in the future. I guarantee you, if you teach Catholic "doctrine" to the catechumens in this way, they will master it and be able to train others in it in ways they will never learn from a textbook or lecture series.

Now you're thinking you don't have a controlled environment like an office and a discrete task like laying out a magazine page. That's true. But it is all the more reason to use the most effective teaching methodology possible. Fortunately, we do have a very effective teaching method and comprehensive structure to make sure we cover everything the catechumens need to become Christians.

USE THE LITURGICAL YEAR

Our comprehensive catechetical structure is the Sundays of the liturgical year. With Sunday as our frame work, here's what an effective catechetical process looks like:

1. Hear the gospel in the context of a faithful Christian community, usually at Sunday Mass.

2. Reflect (out loud, with others) about what that gospel message means for living the Christian life.

3. Compare the reflections of the catechumens to the reflections of the catechist (the teachings of the church) on what the gospel calls us to.

4. Try to live in a new way during the coming week, using the new information from the discussion.

Repeat the process until the whole of the mystery of Christ has been explored. The *minimum* time for that exploration is one full liturgical year. For some, it could take longer.

THE SIX TASKS OF CATECHESIS

As you progress through the liturgical year, you will want to be sure to attend to six different dimensions of the faith life of the catechumens. These six "tasks" are described in the *General Directory for Catechesis* (85).

1. Teach the plan

God has a plan. We know that because Christ *is* the plan. Once we have met Christ, we have the first understanding that God has designed an entire process for our salvation. Our job as catechists is to use the liturgical year to gradually unfold the whole truth of that plan. The *General Directory for Catechesis* points out that the Creed we pray in the liturgy is a summary statement of our faith. Once the catechumens have grasped the fundamental meaning of the Creed, they have come to understand God's plan of salvation for them and for all of creation. (If you open your RCIA to paragraph 157, you'll see that we will make a formal presentation of the Creed to those who will be baptized.)

2. Learn the liturgy

If we are going to get to know Christ, the best place to do that is in the liturgy, particularly in the Sunday assembly. We find the full presence of Christ in the liturgy in a way that surpasses all our other experiences of Christ. A fully active liturgical life is necessary for learning who Christ is. Our job as catechists is to participate fully in the liturgy of the church and to teach the catechumens how to do the same.

3. Walk the talk

If we are going to say we know Jesus, we have to live as though knowing him makes a difference. To *know* him is to do what Jesus would do. For the catechumens, this means turning away from a former lifestyle—a life absent of Christ—and converting to a new way of living. For us Christians, it means a continual recommitment to our new life in baptism. Jesus summed up what this new life looks like in the beatitudes, which, in turn, are an amplification of the Ten Commandments.

4. Practice prayer

As the first disciples were coming to know Jesus, they asked him how they should pray. Jesus' answer, of course, was to teach them the Lord's Prayer, which is the model of all Christian prayer. (Flip over to paragraph 178 in the RCIA for a quick look at the formal presentation of the Lord's Prayer.) The premier experience of prayer for Christians is in the midst of the liturgical assembly, and the catechumens also need to learn how to call on God in prayer in their home life and personal lives. (See TeamRCIA.com for a list of prayers every Catholic should know.)

5. Catechize for community

This can sometimes be a difficult task. In the United States, we put such great importance on our individual resourcefulness that seeing ourselves first of all as members of an interdependent community of love is a challenge. The *General Directory for Catechesis* acknowledges as much and says that the kind of radical community life Jesus calls us to doesn't just happen automatically. It needs to be taught through a process of apprenticeship. The values of Christian community are modeled in the liturgy and lived by the Body of Christ. The job of the catechist is to help the catechumens recognize how the values of the liturgy are evident in the parish community and encourage them to live their own lives in like fashion.

6. Become turnip heads

At the beginning of the book, we used a metaphorical description of turnip heads and how they lived so turnip-like in the world that it made others want to become turnip heads too. The ultimate goal of the initiation process and of the catechist is to train the catechumens to live in society in such a Christian way that others want to become Christians also. It is ultimately what our baptismal vocation is all about. Once we have discerned that the catechumens have mastered this final dimension of catechesis, we can pronounce them ready for election for the Easter sacraments of initiation.

DISCERNMENT OF READINESS

The catechist must continually assess the catechumens' progress in these areas of development by using the four pillars of word, community, worship, and service to determine if the catechumens get it—if there is clear evidence of conversion, if they know enough to live the Christian life.

How will catechists make that assessment? They will do so using a combination of these methods over the entire course of the catechumenate:

1. Watching the actions of the catechumens.

2. Listening to the catechumens' own reflections and assessments.

3. Listening to the stories the sponsors tell about the catechumens.

4. Listening to what the parishioners say (or don't say) about the catechumens.

5. Asking the catechumens direct questions about issues that arise from their worship or their apostolic service.

6. Praying and paying attention to the promptings of the Spirit.

7. Seeking confirmation or assessments from other catechists and the pastor.

And what is it that you are assessing? You are assessing the catechumens' *appropriate* mastery of the four pillars of catechetical formation: word, community, worship, and service.

Word

How well do they know the Scripture stories? Do they know the difference between the Old and New Testaments? Can they identify the four gospels? Can they identify who St. Paul is and why he is important? Can they explain the basics of church teaching that we profess in the Creed? Can they explain the basics of church teaching that we express in the Lord's Prayer? (These are the basic doctrines of the church.)

Community

Do the catechumens know the parish? Do they have friends in the parish who are not part of the catechumenate? Are they familiar with the ministries the parish offers? Do they know the pastor and pastoral staff? Do they understand the parish is part of a diocese and the diocese is part of the universal church? Do they participate in parish events outside the catechumenate?

Worship

Do they participate in Mass every Sunday and other important days of the church? Do they have an active prayer life at home? Do they call upon God in times of distress? Do they recognize that all of life is a gift and regularly offer thanks? Do they know the basic prayers that Catholics pray by heart? (See TeamRCIA.com for a list of prayers every Catholic should know.)

Service

Do the catechumens have a deep concern for the poor and the marginalized in the parish and in the neighborhood? Have they shown evidence of working to alleviate suffering and injustice? Do they have an appropriate grasp of Catholic moral and social teaching?

In making your assessment, you are not looking for Mother Teresas. You are looking for evidence of conversion and a commitment to continue to follow the Cross.

THE ROLE OF SPONSORS IN CATECHESIS

Sponsors are not exactly catechists, but their role in the formation of the catechumens is critical. The sponsors are the folks on the front lines, keeping in touch with the catechumens, monitoring their progress, encouraging them, cajoling them when necessary, and being available to listen to the joys and struggles the catechumens experience as they grow in faith.

Worship

The most important catechetical task a sponsor has is to be sure the catechumen is worshiping with the Sunday assembly each week. The Sunday liturgy is the primary place of formation for the catechumen. If the catechumens are not there every week, they are not being exposed to the full mystery of Christ. And they are not being formed in the fullness of what it means to be Christian.

Word

Participating with the catechumens in the weekly catechetical sessions is next in importance. Many sponsors will "learn" as much as the catechumens, and many will undergo a reconversion to faith. As wonderful as this is, it is not the purpose of their participation in the catechetical sessions. The goal of the catechumenate is the conversion and initiation of the catechumens. Sponsors participate in the catechetical sessions to support this goal. Sponsors who experience a new awakening to their own faith will always be careful not to dominate the conversation and to leave plenty of room for the catechumens to question, explore, and share their faith.

Community

Sponsors will also see to it that the catechumens know about and participate in the activities of the parish. Sponsors will introduce catechumens to the members of the community and will work hard to make sure the catechumens always feel at home in any parish group.

Service

The catechumenate team leader will no doubt schedule occasions for the catechumens to participate in the social ministries of the parish. The sponsor would, of course, participate in the scheduled activities as well. In addition, the sponsors can share with the catechumens how they live out the call to serve the poor and, if appropriate, invite the catechumens to join them in their own ministries of service.

Most of all, a sponsor is a spiritual friend to the catechumen. Sponsors need to meet with the catechumen regularly outside of the catechetical sessions and scheduled events just to ask how things are going. The catechumens will have a lot of questions that they may be too shy to ask in the catechumenate sessions. Sponsors don't need to know all the answers. They need to be able to assure the catechumens that their questions are important and, if the sponsor doesn't know how to answer it at that moment, he will find the answer. Much of the time, no matter what question the catechumens ask, the underlying question, the thing they really want to know, is why do you believe? How does all this make sense to *you*? Are you ever afraid? Do you ever doubt? The sponsor's honest reply to the deeper questions is catechesis in the best sense.

18 Strange and Dangerous Rituals: What You Need to Know about Liturgy

iturgy is dangerous. Why would I say that? I say that because I want you to be careful with it. Liturgy is not a warm and fuzzy experience that can be entered into casually. In liturgy, we enter into the presence of the Holy, and that is always awe-filled. Years ago, Edward Yarnold, SJ, wrote a book titled *The Awe-Inspiring Rites of Initiation.* In his preface, he wrote: "Without being unfaithful to the Greek, I might have called this book 'The Spine-Chilling Rites of Initiation'" (ix). The rites are spine-chilling and awe-filled because our experience of God is so overwhelmingly "other." It cannot be calculated, measured, anticipated, or tamed.

At the same time, liturgy is an immersion in God's love. Now *that* sounds warm and fuzzy, but it really isn't. For many of us, some of our most terrifying and unsettling moments in life had to do with our love lives. Loves we longed for, loves we committed to, loves we lost, loves who demanded we be the best of who we are, loves we did not deserve and yet could not live without.

In worship, we approach the One who loves us most, who loves even what we cannot love about ourselves, and we prostrate ourselves in total gratitude. The spine-chilling love we experience changes us irrevocably. To treat such a love lightly and casually is dangerous not because we will be struck down by an angry God. It is dangerous because we may harden our hearts to the love that can save us from a life of despair.

The catechumens come to us seeking such a love. It is what, in their heart of hearts, they hope they will find in our midst. The liturgy is where they are going to experience the fullness of God's love. The liturgy is where they encounter the sacrificial love of Christ. The way in which we prepare and celebrate the liturgy either will be instrumental in forming them in the spine-chilling awesomeness of that love or will fail to do so and add to their despair. Liturgy is dangerous.

PRINCIPLES FOR RITUAL

Having looked at how we catechize in the RCIA, let's look at how we pray.

Everybody prays…hard

According to the Second Vatican Council, the primary aim to be considered before all else is the full, conscious, and active participation of the assembly. We've all heard that before, right? Well, how are you doing? On a scale of 1 (low) to 10 (high), what is the level of the assembly's participation in the liturgies of your parish? I'm guessing it's 6 or 7. Maybe 8 if you're really on top of things. If it's 9, send me your address. I want to come by and join up. If it's 5 or less, well, you've got a lot of work to do. So let's talk to the 6-7 folks.

Your parish liturgy is pretty good. Not great every Sunday, but you definitely have your moments. Right? Right!

But how do you maximize those moments so the level of participation improves? Are you actively looking for ways to build on what you have? Will you still be a 7 next year, or do you have a plan for becoming an 8?

Moving up a notch

The first principle of good liturgy is that it's not good enough. As soon as you become satisfied with where you are, there is no longer a motivation to improve. If you *are* a 9 on the scale, you probably aren't admitting it. Because if word got around that you thought you were a 9, everyone would take a day off to congratulate themselves. And next thing you know, you'd slip to 8. Parishes that have *great* participation are parishes that are never satisfied with the level they've attained.

ACTION PLAN

1. Evaluate where you are with assembly participation. Be honest. Don't be too hard on yourself, but don't be too easy either. Look especially at the presiding style of all the ministers, the quality of the preaching, the quality of the music, and the efforts the parish makes to be hospitable to strangers at Mass.

2. Get help from your diocesan worship office. If your diocese doesn't have a worship office, call a neighboring diocese that does. You can also find a self-evaluation guide at TeamRCIA.com.

3. Choose one or two areas for improvement in the coming year. Choose a couple of your strong points, not your weak points. It's easier to strengthen what you do well than solve what you struggle with.

4. Set a goal to move up one point on your 10-point scale by this time next year. List specific and measurable actions that will get you there.

Everybody sings

This is a key element of participation. I've heard people say, "I don't sing." Folks, it's not a request. Mass is a sung prayer. It is not a prayer with some singing in it. There are no non-singing roles.

Sure, we all understand that about the folks in the pew. But what about the lectors, you're asking. Their primary role isn't to sing, is it? Lectors are first of all members of the assembly, a singing assembly. In addition, there is a musical component to the ministry of the lector. The lectionary says the readings are enhanced if they are sung, especially the Gospel, as a way of "stirring up the faith of those who hear it" (*Lectionary for Mass*, Introduction, 15).

What about the Communion ministers? They are also primarily ministers of the assembly. And, in their role as Communion ministers, they serve for the entire Communion Rite, that is, from the Lord's Prayer to the Prayer after Communion. They should be actively singing throughout the liturgy, and especially during the Lamb of God, the Communion song (when possible), and the Song after Communion.

And so on. Everybody sings.

WHAT TO LOOK FOR

Is everyone singing the opening song? Are they singing the acclamations in the Eucharistic Prayer? Are they singing as they go to Communion? These are some of the key places in the liturgy by which you can assess the overall singing of the community.

ACTION PLAN

1. Limit the music repertoire used each year so the non-musical people in the parish will be able to learn and sing every song. Twelve to twenty opening songs and five to seven Communion songs, for example, is plenty for most communities.

2. Bring in someone from the diocese or a neighboring diocese to train the cantors in leading music.

3. Hire an organist or pianist who is skilled in liturgical music to help better support the assembly's singing.

4. Make the parish music repertoire part of the parish school and religious education lessons.

5. Ask the presider to chant the opening dialogues to the gospel and the Eucharistic Prayer as well as the preface prayer.

Supersize your symbols

All communication is symbolic, and ritual communication is especially symbolic. The fullest way we can communicate an experience of God is through our ritual symbols. A symbol is a concrete thing (object, word, song) that both points to and is a part of a reality greater than itself. So, for example, the word "God" is a symbol of the unnamable mystery of the divine other. When we use that word, it *symbolizes* a whole lot of meaning, much of which we don't really understand.

Water is another symbol. When we use water ritually, it *symbolizes* many meanings, some of which are simple and some of which are profound. If we use a lot of water, there is clearer communication, more symbolization, of the many meanings of water. If we use only a little water, it symbolizes or "speaks" more quietly, less clearly.

WHAT ARE THE IMPORTANT SYMBOLS?

Anything and everything in ritual is a symbol of something. So what should you focus on? Think of the sacraments and the symbols we use in those, and you'll have a good clue. We call these *primary* symbols. Make the primary symbols big and sensual, and you will go a long way to improving your liturgy. Here's a short list that might not be exhaustive, but it's a good place to begin: water, oil, bread, wine, touch (laying on of hands), light, word, and altar.

The primary symbol in any liturgy is the worshiping assembly, gathered in holy order.

ACTION PLAN

1. Evaluate the primary liturgical symbols in your liturgies. Make a list of at least one thing you can do to improve each one.

2. Ask the catechumens to name the three symbols that stood out for them at last Sunday's Mass. If they are not naming primary symbols, you know you have work to do. If they are naming primary symbols, ask them what they learned about God from their experience of those symbols.

Don't duplicate symbols

This principle is counter-intuitive to North American sensibilities. If one cell phone is good, two is better. Does anybody remember when a two-car family was an anomaly? Some of us even have two houses—one for the winter and one for the summer.

LET THE SYMBOLS SPEAK

In liturgy, as in all art, the opposite is true. The fewer of anything you have generally indicates its greater value and importance. Something that is singular is really special. So in our churches we have one altar, one ambo, one font, and so on.

In the catechumenate rites, this principle sometimes gets overlooked. In the Rite of Acceptance, for example, some parishes present the catechumens with a personal cross or a personal Bible. The duplication of the community cross and the parish lectionary or Book of Gospels dilutes the power of these primary symbols. At first glance having more of them may seem to emphasize cross and word, but in fact it minimizes the power of *the* Cross and *the* Word.

ACTION PLAN

1. Walk through your church, and see if any of the primary symbols are duplicated. Ask yourself if there is a way to emphasize a singular experience of that symbol.

2. Review your catechumenal rites for any duplication of primary symbols. Revise the rites to emphasize the singular power of those symbols.

The homily is an act of faith sharing

The demands of full and active participation do not lessen during the homily. A key liturgical principle is that the homily is an action that flows from and back to the assembly (see *Fulfilled in Your Hearing*, 4). Modern communication theory says that for communication to be effective, the speaker must speak in a way the hearer can understand. The speaker can only know what was heard through an ongoing feedback loop. That means the homilist has to be an integral part of the assembly, constantly dialoguing, sharing, praying, and living with the members of the community. The homily itself is crafted as an act of faith in response to the liturgical "now" the assembly is celebrating.

EVERYBODY WORKS ON THE HOMILY

The members of the assembly are not going to be preaching at Mass. However, they do participate in the homily. We should all come to the liturgy prepared to hear the readings and homily. The people of the parish should be praying over the readings before Mass, forming their questions and insights beforehand so as to have their faith confirmed and challenged, affirmed and argued with in a dynamic interaction on Sunday and throughout the week.

ACTION PLAN

1. Place the reading citations in the Sunday bulletin and the parish Web site along with a weekly faith question. Discuss the question of the week before every parish meeting and encourage families to use it at home. (For a question of the week and a faith sharing guide you can use, go to tinyurl.com/2lvred.)

2. Create a seasonal faith sharing group that includes the parish homilists to pray over and discuss the readings for a liturgical block of time such as Advent.

3. Give regular feedback to the homilists about what touched you and moved you in their preaching. Be specific. Try to tie their preaching to the faith development of the catechumens and the parish community. For example: "Father, when you told that story about _____, I was able to build on that with the catechumens when we were talking about _____."

The lectors proclaim the Word with dignity

Closely linked with the homily is the proclamation of the Word. It goes without saying that lectors (including the deacon or priest) need to practice the readings. But reading the Word goes beyond that. Lectors need to read their reading with the same sense of focus and intensity that the foreman of the jury reads the verdict in a capital case. What the lector does is vital, and it should take every ounce of his focus, energy, and contemplation.

DISCERNING GIFTS

Some people are gifted lectors, and some are not. The goal, of course, is to discern who is gifted and invite those people to serve. But what do you do if there are lectors already on the roster who don't have the gifts? I always encourage people to limit ministers to only one liturgical ministry. So if a lector with secondary skills is also a Communion minister, invite her to limit her service to Communion ministry. (Likewise, if you have a gifted lector who is also a Communion minister, invite him to give up Communion ministry.)

If that isn't an option, spend extra time training the less skilled lectors one-on-one. Most people can be trained to do an acceptable job. It just takes more time, training, and practice.

ACTION PLAN

1. Develop a regular training program for lectors. Spend extra time with the weaker lectors.

2. Get help from the diocesan office.

3. Form a faith-sharing group among the lectors to pray over and practice the readings.

4. Schedule only the very best lectors for the catechumenate rites.

Turn on the lights and speak up

It should go without saying that people need to see and hear. It should. But, it still needs to be said. I was at a Christmas Eve "candlelight" liturgy one year, holding a dark blue song sheet printed with light blue ink. Even if I lit the thing on fire, I don't think there would have been enough light to read it.

CONSERVE THE ENVIRONMENT

I'm as big a fan of creative environment as the next liturgist, but common sense has to come first. If the poinsettias are obscuring the altar or the palm fronds are engulfing the Passion Sunday readers, it's time to reassess. Less is often more in these cases.

ACTION PLAN

1. If any part of your liturgy is outdoors (for example, the Rite of Acceptance, Palm Sunday procession, Easter Vigil fire), be sure the speakers can be heard. Portable sound systems are cheap. Buy, rent, or borrow one.

2. Check the sightlines. Stand in the back of the crowd, sit in the back pew, sit behind one of the pillars. Make adjustments in the choreography of the rite to be sure everyone can see.

3. In larger churches, homilist will often descend from the ambo to preach in closer proximity to the people. The problem is, as soon as he gets down to floor level, he is invisible to two thirds or more of the assembly. The intimacy is increased for him, but diminished for the majority of folks who can no longer see him.

4. In catechumenal rites or other rituals that involve bringing candidates before the assembly, place the subjects of the rite in the aisles throughout the assembly. Everyone in the church can then see the ritual action close up. Yes, it is more work for the ministers. But isn't that why we became ministers? To serve the needs of others?

5. Teach the lectors to project. Even if they have a microphone, it won't do much good without proper public speaking skills.

Respect the liturgical year

The liturgical year is not just a series of Sundays. The structure of the year is a catechetical device that reveals the whole mystery of Christ. That's why catechumens are required to be in the catechumenate for a full liturgical year. They need to experience the entire mystery.

SECOND COLLECTION SUNDAY

We've trained a generation of Catholics to identify the Sundays of the year by whatever group is having their pancake breakfast or award ceremony that day or by whatever cause is being begged for in the second collection. We need to return to a focus on the Sunday as it is identified by the calendar of the church.

ACTION PLAN

1. Pay attention to the transitions between seasons. Usually, the shift from one season to the next is gradual. The readings for the last Sundays of the year, for example, have the same "end times" feel as the first two Sundays of Advent. Instead of abrupt shifts in the environment, plan for gradual evolutions between seasons.

2. Work on a preaching plan that builds from one Sunday to the next and leads the catechumens and the parish into a deeper understanding of the liturgical seasons.

3. Create prayers and activities for the domestic churches in your parish to celebrate the liturgical seasons in their homes.

4. Resist the tendency to honor special groups at the Sunday liturgy. There are national organizations for many of these groups that produce

lots of ritual material for "Cause of the Month Sunday." Just because they wrote intercessions doesn't mean you need to use them. In some dioceses parishes are required to take up second collections for causes such as the Catholic Communications Campaign and the Campaign for Human Development. However, you are not required to rename the Sunday or cede the homily to these worthy causes.

The sound of silence

There is a story we read on the Nineteenth Sunday of Ordinary Time, Year A, about Elijah listening for the voice of God. After several noisy false alarms, he finally hears God's voice in the silence. The way the story is told, Elijah hears some big, powerful force of nature, retreats to silence, hears another force of nature, retreats to silence, and so on, until there is a profound silence in which he hears the voice of God (see 1 Kings 19:9–14, especially the NRSV version).

Be Elijah

In most liturgies I participate in, it is hard to find any silence. And that's a shame. The liturgy is so much more powerful when we attend to the silences. If we use Elijah's story as a model, we can think of the liturgy as an hour-long profound silence, punctuated with powerful speech, powerful song, powerful movement. In a sense, these vocalizations and actions shape the silence to help us know better what to listen for when we return to the silence. Our goal is to get everybody singing, everybody praying, everybody moving *so that,* together, we can enter into the profound silence in which we will experience the mystery of God's presence.

ACTION PLAN

1. In planning and rehearsing the liturgy, plan for the silences.

2. Every Sunday should include significant silences after each reading, after the homily, and after Communion.

3. In the catechumenate rites, plan for significant silences at the Concluding Prayer and the Prayer over the Catechumens in the Rite of Acceptance, the Prayer over the Elect in the Rite of Election, and the laying on of hands in the Scrutiny.

4. The gathering rites and *during* Communion are not appropriate times for silence. These are times for building the sense of community so we can enter the mystery as one.

Move with purpose

Every movement tells a story. We never walk to the altar. We process. We don't shake hands. We share a sign of peace. We bow our heads in prayer, sign ourselves with the cross, offer our hands to receive Communion, and kneel, bow, or prostrate ourselves in supplication, reverence, or repentance. Because every gesture is fraught with meaning, it is jarring when the ministers of the liturgy make offhanded movements that are not part of the script.

WE CATECHIZE WITH OUR BODIES

There is an interesting line in the Rite of Acceptance: "The candidates should be instructed about the celebration of the rite of acceptance" (42). But that's the end of the paragraph. There is no instruction about how to instruct. However, if you think of Christianity more as *doing* something and less as *knowing* something (like we know facts and figures), then the method of instruction becomes obvious. Most of us learned to play baseball by watching the older kids swing the bat, and then we mimicked them. Some of us learned to play a musical instrument the same way. Almost everyone learned to cook by watching and imitating someone else. We learned by moving our bodies in the precise ways required by the thing we were trying to learn. When we moved wrong, we struck out. When we moved right, we got a hit. Liturgy, like ballet or baseball, is a series of right movements.

ACTION PLAN

1. Realize every liturgy is choreographed. Simple liturgies require less choreography, but it is no less important.

2. For any liturgy that is unusual or occasional, such as the catechumenate rites, walk through the rite several times by yourself until you know all the movements that are necessary, until your *body* knows. Then rehearse the other key ministers (not the catechumens) in the movements.

3. Make sure the sponsors move the catechumens the way they need to be moved, when they need to be moved, during the liturgy. The catechumens will learn by doing.

4. In any liturgy, strive to reduce any unnecessary movement. Don't fidget when you sit. Don't walk across the sanctuary if there is no purpose for doing so. Don't sort sheet music or notes. Be a dancer at rest when you are not "on."

PART FIVE

KEEPING IT ALL STRAIGHT

19 Who Will We Meet on the Way?

There is something about the nature of the catechumenate process that attracts just about everyone in the parish who doesn't fit into a neat slot. On the one hand, that is good. You want people in the parish to think of the catechumenate as a place to begin. On the other hand, the catechumenate often becomes a catch-all ministry for folks the parish leadership doesn't otherwise know what to do with. So let's be clear about who the RCIA is "for."

WHO THE RCIA IS FOR

Seekers

A seeker is anyone who is not rooted in faith and is looking for something deeper in their lives. These folks might be baptized or unbaptized. They might be Catholic or not. They are people who have a deep longing, perhaps a longing they are not even fully aware of, and they are drawn to the peace and joy they see in our Catholic communities. As they hang out with Catholics a little and begin to understand a little about our faith in Jesus, one of two things will happen. They will want to know more, or they will decide this Catholic parish is not going to meet their needs at this time. Those who want to know more will eventually wind up in the catechumenate process.

Catechumens

A catechumen is an unbaptized seeker who has undergone a formal shift in status. In the Rite of Acceptance, the seeker declares that she is committed to following the Cross. We, the church, accept that commitment and welcome the catechumen into our community. Catechumens are official members of the church, although they are not yet fully initiated into the community.

Uncatechized candidates for reception or full initiation

A candidate for full initiation is a seeker who is baptized but has never lived a life of faith. These candidates may participate in the catechumenate process with the catechumens, but they *do not* undergo a formal shift in status. They are already baptized, and are already full members of the body of Christ. They may not know that, and they probably haven't lived that way, but that does not affect their status. They are Christians. Nothing can change that.

These candidates can be either Catholics who were never fully initiated or non-Catholics. Their faith journey will be similar to that of the catechumens, but we must never confuse them.

What is crucial to keep in mind about these seekers is that they are truly seekers. They have never lived a life of faith and do not realize the saving power of Christ.

WHO THE RCIA IS NOT FOR

Fallen-away Catholics

These are seekers who have been fully initiated, have lived a life of faith at some point in their life, and have lost their way. They are now on the road back to rediscover the faith they once knew. These folks would *not* be part of the catechumenate, but they could very well be part of a similar process that parallels many of the steps of the catechumenate.

The under-catechized faithful

This is where the initiation ministry can get cluttered. Our parishes are filled with Catholics who do not know their faith well, whose participation in Mass is spotty, and whose lifestyles do not vibrantly reflect gospel values. Nevertheless, they have been raised in the faith, usually come to Communion when they are at Mass, and know how they are *supposed* to live. Many of these folks show up when they want to get married or have a baby baptized. Sometimes they are not confirmed. A light goes off in a staff member's head: "Confirmation is a sacrament of initiation. This person needs to be in the RCIA."

Wrong. Our current practice of confirmation is varied. Even if our theology tells us it is a sacrament of initiation, our practice of celebrating confirmation after first Communion says something different. Someone who has celebrated their first Communion can't get anymore "initiated" since Eucharist is the pinnacle of our sacramental life. These under-catechized members of the community need a renewal process, and for those who are not confirmed, that process could lead to confirmation. But that renewal process is rooted in a life of faith, not a first discovery of faith. The under-catechized Catholics need their own process and do not belong in the catechumenate process.

Faithful Protestants

This is another group that gets lumped into the catechumenate, and we really need to clean up our act about this. Those who were baptized in another ecclesial tradition and have lived faithfully in that tradition *are already catechized and fully initiated.* What they are *not* is in full communion with the Roman Catholic Church. When they seek to become part of our community, they are not doing so because they are seeking faith. They are already part of the faithful. They are seeking a fuller expression of that faith, and they are seeking full communion with us. But that certainly does not require a year-long process with all the conversion therapies and faith-building processes of the catechumenate. The National Statutes for the Catechumenate recognize this: "Those baptized persons who have lived as Christians and need only instruction in the Catholic tradition and a degree of probation within the Catholic community should not be asked to undergo a full program parallel to the catechumenate" (31). A baptized Christian who has been participating in parish life with his Catholic spouse for many years, even raising his children as Catholics, might need only some instruction in the Catholic tradition and "a degree of probation" (faith sharing, a spiritual retreat, reconciliation) lasting only a few weeks. Each case needs to be discerned individually. But in no case would a person such as this participate in the catechumenate (except, perhaps, as a catechist!).

Interested tourists

I often hear folks who have been sponsors or catechists on catechumenate teams say: "I think every Catholic should go through the RCIA! It's such a wonderful experience!" It is a wonderful experience, and it is a powerful source of renewal for Catholic team members. But it is not *for* them. The church has many renewal processes for Catholics, and we need to make fuller use of them. The primary source of renewal is the Sunday liturgy. Closely linked to the liturgy is the ongoing adult catechetical process of the parish. If the liturgical and catechetical efforts of the parish are not generating ongoing renewal, the parish needs to put more effort there. The catechumenate has other work to do.

CHILDREN

Children fall into most of the previous categories, and they should usually be ministered to with a process similar to adults, but adapted to their age level. (We'll discuss adapting the rite for children more in chapter 20.) Unfortunately, what too often happens is children who are seeking faith are ministered to in the same way as the other Catholic children in the parish. Here are a few things to take note of.

Unbaptized children

Unbaptized children follow the same initiation process as unbaptized adults. Once children have reached catechetical age, they go through all the stages of the catechumenate: inquiry, catechumenate, purification and enlightenment, mystagogy.

When child catechumens are ready to be initiated, they are initiated at the Easter Vigil and they celebrate all three sacraments of initiation: baptism, confirmation, and Eucharist. There can be no exception to this. It is the universal teaching of the church, and not even a bishop is free to deviate from this practice. (See Code of Canon Law, 852 and RCIA, 305.)

Many dioceses and catechetical programs define catechetical age as seven years or older. This is not precisely correct. "Catechetical age" is a new term that was introduced when the RCIA was published. It means roughly the same thing as "age of discretion," which is the term used in canon law and other sacramental rites. Historically, the "age of discretion" is the age when one can tell the difference between right and wrong. Most children can make that distinction by the time they are seven years old. Some children, however, can make the distinction between right and wrong at a younger age and would therefore be of "catechetical age." The determination of catechetical age is based on the spiritual maturity of the child and not on his chronological age.

Baptized, non-Catholic children

Usually Protestant children who wish to be in full communion with the Catholic Church are following the wishes of their parents who are also seeking full communion. The ministry to these children would follow the pattern of ministry to their parents.

Parents

When parents bring children to us for initiation, we need to think of the process as a ministry to the family. And that family ministry should focus primarily on the adults and secondarily on the children. Even if the parents are already baptized, they have not been living their faith fully or else their children would already be baptized. Our ministry efforts need to focus on developing the faith lives of the parents and leading them to deeper conversion. Without that, there is little chance their children will grow up practicing the faith. So, in reality, the children are not "ready" for initiation until their parents are. There are always exceptions, of course, and each family needs to be dealt with according to their own needs.

20 You Have to Be "This High" to Ride: Children and the RCIA

L et's get this right out on the table. If you search Amazon.com for "RCIC," or "Rite of Christian Initiation of Children," nothing useful will come up. There is no such book. There is no such rite.

But what about all those children we baptized last year at the Easter Vigil, you're asking.

Ah, those weren't children. Those were adults. Flip to the very back of your RCIA, and find the National Statutes for the Catechumenate. Then look for paragraph 18:

> Since children who have reached the use of reason are considered, for purposes of Christian initiation, to be adults (canon 852:1), their formation should follow the general pattern of the ordinary catechumenate as far as possible, with the appropriate adaptations permitted by the ritual. They should receive the sacraments of baptism, confirmation, and eucharist at the Easter Vigil, together with the older catechumens.

So there is no RCIC (or RCIT or RCIY)—only the RCIA. The children are considered adults in the sense that the RCIA is the appropriate ritual for them as opposed to the Rite of Baptism, which is for infants. We use the RCIA, and we adapt it for children. So how do we do that?

ADAPTING THE RITE FOR CHILDREN

Something strange happens to us when we deal with children. I can't quite account for it. Perhaps if I had children of my own, I'd understand better. As it is, I can only tell you some of the things I observe.

133

One thing I see a lot of, which I'm sure you see too, is the kiss'n'drop syndrome. Parents bring their kids to the parish school or the director of religious education, kiss them goodbye, and come back six to eight years later hoping they have been turned into good Catholics.

On the other side of coin, I see teachers and catechists accepting this burden as though Jesus had personally asked them, all by themselves, to rescue these children from a life of spiritual darkness to which they must surely be doomed if the catechists don't step in. As a result, they try to cram as much religious education as they can into the short amount of time they have with the unfortunate waifs. Their hope is that someday all this information might "take," and the children will be grateful.

Okay, now here's the really strange part. If I ask any of these spiritually absent parents if they really think their children will learn the faith from a near-stranger, one hour a week, they answer along the lines of it's better than nothing, but no, not really.

And if I ask the catechists if they really think the little ones will grow up with deep faith without any kind of support at home, no matter how heroic their own efforts are, they answer about the same way.

This odd behavior seems to be exacerbated in families who have not had their children baptized by the time they reach catechetical age and catechists who are pressed into service to start or lead a children's catechumenate. Perhaps parents who have been so disconnected from church they could not meet even the minimal requirements for infant baptism are even more insecure about their ability to teach their children the faith. And perhaps the catechists feel an added burden of preparing children not just for first Communion but, maybe, for their entire salvation.

INITIAL DISCERNMENT

Anyway, as I said, it doesn't make much sense to me. Here's what makes sense to me. When mom and dad, or grandma, or crazy Aunt Judith brings Johnny to us to get his sacraments, the first question has to be, why are you here?

"I just told you. Johnny needs his sacraments," say mom and dad.

"Why?" I might ask.

And then, we would go from there. If mom and dad think you, or I, or the church, or God want Johnny to get his sacraments, like getting all his vaccinations, we need to, in our kindest, most pastoral way, let the parents know that doesn't make any sense. Unless the whole family is growing in faith together, it isn't going to make much sense to pack Johnny off on a journey to the Cross all by himself.

I truly believe that when it comes to adapting the rite for children, the biggest adaptation we have to make is to pay more attention to the parents than the kids. Now don't panic. We're not going to ignore the children. But our focus has to be on their primary catechists—the parents. We are going to use the rites and the catechetical process for children to draw the parents into a conversion journey.

FAMILY AFFAIR

So, on the first encounter, we need to think of the *family* as inquirers. The decision about the readiness of children to enter the catechumenate will not be based on the child's individual readiness. We are saying that if the adults, or at least one of the primary caretakers in the family, are not ready, the children are not ready. Just as with adult inquirers, we are *not* refusing to celebrate the sacraments with the children. We are inviting the family to spend some more time with us, reflecting more deeply on what they really want. We pray that in that process the Spirit will move them to the initial faith needed to celebrate the Rite of Acceptance. However, we cannot promise them a certain date on which that will happen.

What if they leave? I don't know what will happen if they leave. I know what *won't* happen. God will not abandon them and especially will not abandon the children. God only asked one of us to be the savior, and it wasn't me. Jesus' saving presence is with all of God's children, all the time.

I also know what *will* happen if we just go through the sacramental motions with the children who live in families with little or no faith. We will add to the family's cynicism about the rites, confirming their suspicions that all this church mumbo jumbo is meaningless anyway.

What makes most sense for the kiss'n'drop families is some sacramental tough love. In our best pastoral voice, we are going to offer the families an opportunity to grow in their faith along with their children. We are going to ask them to participate in the full inquiry and catechumenate process, right along with their children, for however long it takes for the family to be ready (review chapter 5 for more about readiness). If mom and dad are unable to participate at this time, we should be happy to accept their children into the regular parish religious education process. But we need to be clear with the parents that one of the criteria for initiation means a readiness on the part of the children's primary catechists to accompany their children through the catechumenate. If mom and dad (or another caretaker) are not ready, the child cannot possibly be ready.

Okay, now, before you start dragging out all the baptismal photos of children who are an exception to the rule, yes, there are extraordinary children or extraordinary circumstances that might cause us to overlook a requirement that the parents be actively involved in this important phase of their children's lives. But "extraordinary" is just that. Our *ordinary* response has to place the responsibility for the faith life of the children squarely on their parents' shoulders.

WHO ARE THESE CHILDREN?

Open your copy of the RCIA to paragraph 252. Paragraphs 252 to 259 are critically important for catechumenate teams that are going to work with children, and you should proceed no further until you have a thorough understanding of this section of the rite.

What's the minimum age?

The adaptations here are normally intended for "children, not baptized as infants, who have attained the use of reason and are of catechetical age" (252). What age is that? I don't know. I haven't met the children in question. I would have to talk with them to find out if they could reason and if they were able to be catechized. For some children, that might be a very young age. For other children, it might be older. The age at which children move from "infants" to "catechetical age" cannot be determined ahead of time. (See also the sidebar on page 131.)

Be careful not to become fixated on age seven as a magic age. Canon law and many diocesan guidelines indicate that most children have reached the age of reason by age seven. But it is not intended as an absolute determination, only as a guideline. Some children could be younger, and a few might be older.

What's the maximum age?

At what age are children too old for these adaptations? That also cannot be determined without speaking to the children in question. As a general guideline, if a child is capable of making other important life decisions on his own—such as what electives to study in school, what things to buy with his own money, how and when he will do his homework, for example—the closer he is to being treated more like an adult and less like a child. It's a judgment call for each individual.

The prime directive is given in the last sentence of paragraph 252: "[Children who are subjects of these adaptations] cannot yet be treated as adults because, at this stage of their lives, they are dependent on their parents or guardians and are still strongly influenced by their companions and their social surroundings."

What are the steps?

Read paragraph 253. The process and the steps are the same as with the adults.

INQUIRY

Children must undergo a process of conversion before they can be admitted to the catechumenate. It is important that mom and dad also undergo a conversion journey. So while the children are in an inquiry process, so are their parents.

For the children, the inquiry environment could very well be the parish religious education program. Remember, they are "still strongly influenced by their companions and their social surroundings." If you have an effective catechetical process in your parish, surrounding the inquirers with believers of similar age can be a positive influence on their conversion. Also read paragraph 254.1.

At the same time, if their parents are immersed in the adult inquiry process, their conversion process can also have a positive impact on the children. Also read through paragraph 254.2.

Always keep in mind this is the stage at which the children (and their parents) get to set the agenda. They ask the questions and set the pace. We cannot place our agenda on top of their seeking. They may not ultimately choose to pursue initiation in your parish. As we mentioned above, the conversion process might not fit with their preconceptions of what "getting the sacraments" looks like. We have to accept that as part of their inquiry process, and not prematurely move their children into the catechumenate. Conversion always precedes initiation.

CATECHUMENATE

The catechumenate process for children has the same goal as it does for adults:

> The catechumenate is an extended period…aimed at training [the catechumens] in the Christian life. (75)

There will be two strong influences on children to help train them in Christian living. As we have said, those influences are their peers and their parents.

The rite suggests that the catechumenate process for children *is* the catechetical process for "children of the same age who are already baptized and are preparing for confirmation and eucharist…" (254.1). The rite goes on to suggest that the child catechumens should "come to the sacraments of initiation at the same time that their baptized companions are to receive confirmation or eucharist" (256).

What's wrong with this picture?

There are some difficulties with this vision that we have to sort through.

Most significant is the assumption in the RCIA that the baptized children are going to be confirmed before or in conjunction with their first Communion. That happens in a few dioceses in the U.S., but most Catholic children celebrate first Communion around age seven and confirmation three to ten years later.

The RCIA also assumes the baptized children are in a process that uses mystagogical catechesis, flowing from the celebration of the Sunday liturgy. Again, this happens in some parishes, particularly those who are engaged in a whole community catechesis model of faith formation. But if your parish uses a classroom model of formation, that could be detrimental to child catechumens who are new to the faith.

Finally, trying to time the readiness of the catechumens to match that of their baptized peers seems impossibly artificial. The readiness of the catechumens for initiation is dependent upon many factors, primarily those we discussed in the section on the adult catechumenate found in paragraph 75 of the rite. The readiness of their baptized peers might be an additional factor to consider, but it cannot be the driving force.

It's catechumenate time. Do you know where your parents are?

The parents or guardians need to be in an ongoing catechetical process also. Part of your determination to accept the children into the catechumenate is a discernment of their parents' readiness to follow the Cross and learn to live as Christians along with their children. If the parents are going to be true catechists for their children, they need to be catechized themselves. It seems reasonable to expect at least one of the children's guardians to participate in the catechetical sessions with the adult catechumens during the length of their children's catechumenate.

PURIFICATION AND ENLIGHTENMENT

Just as with the adult catechumens, this is a period of spiritual preparation for the child catechumens. Do not be tempted to use it as a time to catch up with "lessons" they have missed. The discernment for readiness for the child catechumens to move to this stage is similar to that of the adult catechumens. You will want to discern how well they have integrated the four pillars of catechesis (for their ages) as outlined in paragraph 75: word, community, worship, and service. See paragraph 120 of the RCIA as a good review of the markers of readiness.

Are mom and dad ready?

The difference between discerning readiness of adults and children is that with the child catechumens an additional discernment of their parents' readiness is also necessary. If the child catechumen does not have an adult guardian who has also fully integrated the Christian lifestyle of word, community, worship, and service, there is little hope the child will grow up living a fully Christian life.

MYSTAGOGY

After their initiation, we expect to see the young neophytes and their parents at the Sunday liturgies of the Easter season. This is the "main setting" of their post-baptismal catechesis (paragraph 247). Homilists need to take this into account, and they may want to consult with members of the catechumenate team who are skilled at speaking in ways children understand.

Preach to the parents

Even though the children are the neophytes, the homily should be primarily directed to the adults. Children can understand good preaching, even when it is an "adult" homily. Don't water it down or, worse, take a "time out" to speak exclusively to the children. Give the parents something to chew on that they can explore more deeply with their children after Mass.

Do the liturgy well

The homily is not the only or even the main catechetical moment of the liturgy. Children will be catechized much more deeply by the non-verbal, symbolic elements of the rite. Take another look at the liturgical principles section of this book (chapter 18), and make sure the liturgies of the Easter season are the finest of the year in your parish.

Sponsors

During the inquiry period, as you start thinking about sponsors for the child catechumens, keep in mind the distinction between sponsors and godparents (see chapter 6). You can be a little more creative in choosing sponsors than you can with godparents. For example, you might designate someone from your sponsor pool to serve as the sponsor for an entire family. She would then mentor the parents in serving in a sponsor-like role for their children. Both the parish sponsor and parents would accompany the child catechumens in the rites and through the catechetical process.

> Technically speaking, the rules for who can be a sponsor and a godparent are the same. However, as long as you have one sponsor who fulfills the canonical requirements, you can have any number of other folks who are "in company" with the Catholic sponsor. See Canon 874.

You might also consider asking a parish family to sponsor an inquiring family. So a mom and dad with two or three children might sponsor a similar family who is seeking to have their children initiated.

Finally, if you have enough people available, you might try to find individual sponsors for each child. An individual sponsor might be more important especially for older children who are beginning to show some independence from their parents. A mature teenage parishioner could be a good choice to be a sponsor in this case.

Godparents

To be a godparent, the minimum requirements are that he or she must be fully initiated, a practicing Catholic, and at least sixteen years of age. (Check with your diocesan office, though. Your bishop may have designated a different minimum age.) Only one godparent is required but the child may have two. If there are two, one needs to be a man and the other a woman. You cannot have two men or two women.

But those are just the *minimum* requirements. The *Catechism of the Catholic Church* says "the godfather and godmother…must be firm believers, able and ready to help the newly baptized—child or adult—on the road of Christian life" (1255). So being a godparent is a lifelong role and not something to be taken on lightly.

Padrinos and madrinas

In some cultural traditions, different sets of godparents are asked to serve for each of the initiation sacraments, baptism, confirmation, and Eucharist. Strictly speaking, the child can only have two godparents, not six. However, other *padrinos* and *madrinas* can be asked to serve as "witnesses" to the child's initiation. Their commitment can be as formal and solemn as the "official" godparents. They are simply not listed in the parish baptismal register as the godparents.

Liturgies with children

For those who are planning liturgies with children, it is essential to read the Directory for Masses with Children. You can find this in the front of the sacramentary. You can also find it online (tinyurl.com/2wu8hc). The Directory points out that even though children may not fully understand everything that happens at Mass, they are very good at understanding some important Christian behaviors.

> These values include
> the community activity,
> exchange of greetings,
> capacity to listen and to seek and grant pardon,
> expression of gratitude,
> experience of symbolic actions,
> a meal of friendship,
> and festive celebration. (9)

The Directory goes on to point out that children learn these values best in the context of their families. So you will want to pay attention to two things in planning the rites with children:

1. Go to lengths to make sure these values are highlighted in the liturgy.

2. Be sure the parents understand when these moments occur so they can discuss them with their children after the liturgy.

If your parish has a separate liturgy of the word for the baptized children of the parish, you will want to forgo this and keep all the children with the main assembly on days when you celebrate catechumenate rituals. The rites of the catechumenate are highly catechetical in themselves, and the children of the parish should not miss out on them.

Lots of adults, lots of kids

The Directory speaks of two kinds of Masses with children. The first is a Mass for adults at which there are a large number of children. This is what most parishes refer to as a "Family Mass." Or it may just be the 10 AM Mass in your parish that lots of families happen to attend. This type of liturgy is always a liturgy focused on adults but accommodated as far as possible to the participation of the children.

> Nevertheless, in Masses of this kind it is necessary to take great care that the children present do not feel neglected because of their inability to participate or to understand what happens and what is proclaimed in the celebration. Some account should be taken of their presence: for example, by speaking to them directly in the introductory comments (as at the beginning and the end of Mass) and at some point in the homily. (17)

It will be at a liturgy like this that rituals such as the Rite of Acceptance and the Scrutinies are celebrated.

Lots of kids, few adults

The Directory then deals with liturgies *for* children, at which there are a few adults present. Typically, this is a school Mass or a liturgy for the religious education program on a weekday. The Directory offers several adaptations that might be made at these liturgies. It cautions us, however, to maintain the Sunday liturgy as the children's primary liturgical experience:

> It is always necessary to keep in mind that these Eucharistic celebrations must lead children toward the celebration of Mass with adults, especially in the Masses at which the Christian community must come together on Sundays. (21)

It is at school or weekday liturgies such as these where the child catechumens might experience a minor exorcism or blessing or might be presented with the Lord's Prayer and the Creed.

PRINCIPLES

The Directory for Masses with Children lists several principles in the section titled "Masses with Children in Which only a Few Adults Participate" that are really applicable to any liturgy. It will be helpful for liturgy planners to read through these with an eye toward incorporating some of these values into the Sunday liturgies at which the catechumenal rites are celebrated with children. Pay particular attention to these:

Participation is primary

> The principles of active and conscious participation are in a sense even more significant for Masses celebrated with children. Every effort should therefore be made to increase this participation and to make it more intense. (22)

On Sunday, we cannot go as far as the Directory suggests for children's Masses. Turning the Sunday liturgy into a children's Mass actually lessens overall participation. However, the principle is important to note. There are many things we can do at a Sunday liturgy to increase the participation of both children and adults.

Good presiding

> It is the responsibility of the priest who celebrates with children to make the celebration festive, familial, and meditative....
>
> The priest should be concerned above all about the dignity, clarity, and simplicity of his actions and gestures. In speaking to the children he should express himself so that he will be easily understood, while avoiding any childish style of speech. (23)

This is just as true in liturgies with adults. I sometimes hear complaints that a given parish's pastor simply isn't good with children. Most often I've found that a little rehearsal goes a long way toward improving rapport with children. If your pastor truly is unable to turn on the charm with the little ones, give him a ritual assistant who can help him with the children during the rite.

Good preaching

> With the consent of the pastor or rector of the church, one of the adults may speak to the children after the gospel, especially if the priest finds it difficult to adapt himself to the mentality of children. (24)

This is an adaptation that is allowed at weekday Masses with children, but not at Sunday Masses. However, using the underlying principle, the children's catechist might summarize the homilist's words for the benefit of the children. This would have to be well planned and rehearsed ahead of time so the assembly doesn't feel like they're hearing a second sermon just for the children.

Good music

> Singing must be given great importance in all celebrations, but it is to be especially encouraged in every way for Masses celebrated with children, in view of their special affinity for music. (30)

Again this should be a principle observed as much in adult liturgies as it is in children's liturgies. If the parish repertoire consistently focuses on good music children can sing (as opposed to children's music), you will have no trouble excelling at this value. Don't get caught in the trap of doing simplistic music for the sake of the children. Most children are quite capable of handling some fairly sophisticated repertoires. If you don't believe me, slip over to the neighboring Baptist or Lutheran parish some Sunday and listen to the complex melodies and harmonies their children are singing.

Shhhhh

> Even in Masses with children "silence should be observed at the designated times as part of the celebration…." (37, General Instruction of the Roman Missal, 45)

There is a big difference between "being quiet" and ritual silence. Children know the difference. I'm not always sure adults do. Adults are sometimes quiet so as not to disturb others, such as in a library or walking into church. Children seem to know instinctively when there is nothing really going on in the silence and feel free to break it, much to the chagrin of their parents. However, when there is something actively happening in the silence, when the Spirit is moving, children know. Provide lots of space in the liturgy for the Spirit to move within the assembly and for the children to teach us how to pay attention.

Ritual adaptations

In case you haven't caught on yet, I am obsessive about referring to the RCIA when we speak about the pastoral implementation of the initiation process. But there's an exception to everything, right? Here's mine. I don't think the ritual adaptations for children in the RCIA are our best option.

WHAT DOES THE RITE SAY?

If you open to the table of contents in the RCIA you will see two parts. Part I is the normative rite for adults. Everything there is based on the universal rite that the entire church follows.

Part II is a set of adaptations for particular circumstances. Most of these adaptations are optional. So here's my exception to the rule. When it comes to the optional adaptations, I am not a fan. They seem to obscure the entire purpose of the normative rites. This is particularly the case with the adaptations for children.

My discomfort with the children's adaptations is crystallized in paragraph 257: "For children of this age, at the rites during the process of initiation, it is generally preferable not to have the whole parish community present, but simply represented."

My experience has been just the opposite. Children, sometimes more than the adults, enter enthusiastically into the full celebration of the rites. There may be an exception here and there, but it can't be said that as a general rule children shouldn't go through the same ritual celebrations as the adults with the entire parish community present. The rest of the ritual adaptations following 257 flow from the premise that the rites should be minimized for children, and so I don't find the adaptations helpful. Refer instead to the rites in Part I and the principles from the Directory for Masses with Children, and give the child catechumens the fullest experience possible.

WHAT ELSE DOES THE RITE SAY?

There are some adaptations of the ritual that are optional (260-303) and some elements of the ritual that are not adaptations of the normative rite and are not optional. Specifically, when we get to the liturgy of initiation itself, the rite says:

> At this third step of their Christian initiation,
> the children will receive the sacrament of baptism,
> the bishop or priest who baptizes them will also confer confirmation,
>   and the children will for the first time
> participate in the liturgy of the eucharist. (305)

In other words, confirmation and Eucharist are not optional. Unbaptized children who have reached catechetical age can only be initiated in this way—celebrating baptism, confirmation, and Eucharist in the same celebration. It doesn't matter what your diocesan age for confirmation is. This rule is part of canon law and supersedes diocesan policy. Not even your bishop is free to deviate from this. If your pastor is the one doing the baptism, he automatically has permission to confirm the child. No special delegation from the bishop is needed (323). And, of course, he would give the child first Communion at the same liturgy.

Because of the varied practice of when to confirm in the United States, the U.S. bishops wanted to be exceedingly clear about this. So they wrote the National Statutes for the Catechumenate, which you will find in the appendix to your RCIA. If you look at paragraphs 18-19 in that document, you will find even stronger language reinforcing the norm of celebrating all three initiation sacraments at the same time.

21 Welcoming the Baptized

W hen I first started learning about the catechumenate process, the only people I knew who wanted to become Catholic were Lutherans. These were hymn-singing, Bible quoting, Minnesota Lutherans who were worshipping at Mass with us almost every Sunday. The reason they were at Mass is because they were married to Catholics. Most of them had children they were raising as Catholics. Because they had to go to parent preparation meetings when they wanted to baptize their children or help prepare them for first Communion, some of these Lutherans knew Catholic teaching better than some cradle Catholics.

And, as God is my witness, we made them go through the entire catechumenate when they finally decided to become Catholic. Unfortunately, this still happens in too many places. And it is not what the rite intends.

CONVERSION

We said in chapter 1 that the RCIA is a transmogrification machine. It changes a non-believer into a believer. Folks who have already been transmogrified and are living out their faith are not subjects for the RCIA.

Nevertheless, here are some of the arguments that some catechumenate ministers give (and that I've given in my disreputable past) for putting these baptized candidates through the catechumenate process.

"It's good for them"

The initiation process is deeply spiritual, and all those associated with it are moved to a deeper level of faith. This has happened to you and me, and it's a key reason we continue in this ministry. We've all heard lifelong, faithful Catholics who wind up serving as sponsors gush like teenagers about how their faith has never seemed so alive before. So what can be the harm in providing such a powerful renewal process for the baptized candidates?

The harm is we lose sight of the original purpose of the rite. The RCIA is a sacrament of initiation for those who have never been baptized. The structure and language of the rites are designed to move a person from unbelief to belief. When we put the baptized candidates through the RCIA, we are saying, in a not-so-subtle way, that their initiation was somehow lacking and now needs to be filled out. Never mind that this is not very complimentary to the Lutheran Church (or Baptist, or Presbyterian, etc.). It is also heresy. When someone is baptized, in any Christian tradition, it is God who acts, not us. And God's action cannot be partial, incomplete, or undone. Baptized is baptized.

"They are completing their initiation"

Okay, we believe baptized is baptized, but that's just step one, right? Well, yes and no. For many Christian traditions, baptism means full initiation. For Catholics, you have to also be confirmed and receive Eucharist to be fully initiated. But this raises a problem. If a Lutheran (or Baptist, or Presbyterian, etc.), who believes he is a fully initiated Christian, wants to become a Catholic, we immediately begin using the language of "completing" his initiation.

Now, obviously, these folks are drawn to the Catholic faith because they find a fuller expression of their Christianity in our tradition. But how do we respect their baptism and their life of faith up to now without equating them with catechumens?

Paul Turner discusses this question at length in his book *When Other Christians Become Catholic* (Pueblo). Turner makes the point that these folks are not at the beginning of their journey.

> If baptism is a beginning, the rite of reception [of baptized Christians into the full communion of the Catholic Church] is not. It meets people midstream in the Christian crossing. Celebrating the rite of reception with integrity requires a unique spiritual formation distinct from the prebaptismal catechumante. Preparation for it begins in the middle of life in Christ, not at the beginning. (15)

Turner points out that baptized Christians of other traditions are *already* in communion with Catholics although that communion is incomplete. He cites the Catechism, which says: "Baptism constitutes the foundation of communion among all Christians, including those who are not yet in *full communion...*" (1271, emphasis added).

So in one sense, the Lutherans (etc.) among us are completing their initiation. But a more ecumenical view that is more respectful of their baptismal status might be that they are coming into full communion.

"They'll feel left out"

Gosh, we even hear cradle Catholics saying this, don't we? Inevitably, someone from the middle pews gets swept up into the catechumenate process as a sponsor or volunteer and a couple of weeks before the Easter Vigil says something like, "I wish I hadn't been baptized as an infant so I could go through all these rites as an adult."

It just breaks my heart when I hear things like that. I've had my share of ups and downs with my Catholic faith, but I can't imagine any scenario in which my life would have been *better* if I had not been baptized as a baby. It's like saying I wish I hadn't met my mom until I was an adult.

When the Lutherans (etc.) want to become Catholic, our first response has to be a joyful acclamation of the baptized life they have already been leading. If our language and our practice indicates they have been missing something—as the catechumens indeed have—and that they will feel "left out" if we place them among the baptized Catholics instead of the unbaptized catechumens, we are doing serious harm to their catechesis and their sense of their baptismal dignity.

"We don't have any catechumens"

If there are no catechumens this year, some parishes argue, we won't have anyone to celebrate the initiation rites with. I once heard liturgical theologian Kathleen Hughes reply to this argument. She wondered if a parish had no one die that year, would they choose someone from the parish to do the funeral rites to so they could celebrate that beautiful ritual?

Remember always to look at the introduction to a rite you intend to celebrate and find its primary purpose. If we celebrate a rite for secondary reasons, it will miscatechize the candidates and the community.

"They are uncatechized"

This is the strongest argument for placing baptized Christians in the catechumenate. It is bolstered by the RCIA itself. Turn to Part II:4, "Preparation of Uncatechized Adults for Confirmation and Eucharist" (400):

> The following pastoral guidelines concern adults who were baptized as infants either as Roman Catholics or as members of another Christian community but did not receive further catechetical formation nor, consequently, the sacraments of confirmation and eucharist.

The rest of this section of the RCIA goes on to provide optional rites for the uncatechized, baptized candidates that are modeled on the rites for the catechumens in Part I.

What we have to keep in mind here is that while the catechesis of these folks may be deficient, their baptism is not, as we said above. The RCIA also presses this point:

> Even though uncatechized adults have not yet heard the message of the mystery of Christ, their status differs from that of catechumens, since by baptism they have already become members of the Church and children of God. (400)

Okay, get your highlighters ready:

> Hence their conversion is based *on the baptism they have already received*... (emphasis added).

It seems to me that if we are going to catechize baptized people on the baptism they have already received, that catechesis is going to be intrinsically different from the prebaptismal catechesis of the catechumens.

Sure, a lot of what we do with the catechumens will look a lot like what we do with the uncatechized, baptized candidates. But that is all the more reason to have baptized candidates in a different process from the catechumens. If the candidates and catechumens are celebrating similar rituals and engaging in a similar small-group faith formation process, it becomes one more catechetical challenge to continually point out the intrinsic differences between the two groups. The extrinsic differences are sometimes so subtle so as to go unnoticed by the candidates themselves and, indeed, most Catholic parishioners who still think of Protestants-becoming-Catholics as "converts."

BUT ARE THEY REALLY UNCATECHIZED?

Another difficulty that arises in many places is the blurring of distinctions between catechized and uncatechized. We can all use more catechesis, right? Of course we can! That's why our parishes are urged to focus on adult formation as a central and ongoing process for the entire community. Given that we are engaged in lifelong catechesis, the catechetical standard for the full communion of baptized Christians is fairly simple. They need to have an appropriate (beginner-level) understanding of the elements in paragraph 75: word, community, worship, and service. The National Statutes emphasize this point.

> Those baptized persons who have lived as Christians and need only instruction in the Catholic tradition and a degree of probation within the Catholic community should not be asked to undergo a full program parallel to the catechumenate. (31)

Notice the standard is not "lived as *perfect* Christians." If the baptized person has been negligent in living the Christian life—as most of us have been at one time or another—but knows how she *should be* living, the problem isn't lack of catechesis. The problem is temptation and sin, the normal remedy for which is a penitential return to the baptismal lifestyle.

"We don't have enough volunteers"

This one is the show-stopper. It has been for me, that's for sure. If you are in a small community (or even a large one), you just might not have the person power to facilitate both an initiation process for the unbaptized and a full communion process for the baptized. I've been in that situation, and I made compromises to save my sanity and provide as much spiritual and catechetical support as I could to those who wanted to become Catholic. Even so, I held myself to some principles.

The first principle was to keep rites for the catechumens separate from and scheduled on different Sundays from the rites for the baptized candidates. This was a fairly easy goal to meet since we were at Mass every Sunday anyway. And it made a clear distinction between the two groups.

The second principle was to make the rites for the baptized candidates look markedly different from the rites for the catechumens and to take into account the baptized's status as full members of the worshipping assembly. For example:

- We went outside to greet the catechumens for the Rite of Acceptance, but we started inside for the baptized candidates (because the baptized are already members of the church) when ritualizing the beginning of their process.
- We signed the catechumens with the cross but did not sign the bap-

tized candidates. They're already marked with the cross because of their baptism.

- The baptized candidates were not dismissed from Mass with the catechumens.

- The baptized candidates participated in the scrutinies as members of the assembly, not as subjects of the rite. (There is no option for scrutinies for the baptized, yet some parishes lump them in anyway.)

- The reception into full communion usually took place at a Sunday Mass, not the Easter Vigil. (We made exceptions for those who had unbaptized relatives being initiated at the Vigil.)

None of this requires any more volunteers than you would need if you did the combined rites for catechumens and candidates (Appendix I of the RCIA).

The place where we needed more volunteers was during the catechetical sessions. We simply didn't have enough catechists to run two different catechetical processes. Nor did we have enough catechists to provide for ongoing formation for the Catholic parishioners. So we gathered *everybody* together for catechesis—Catholics, Lutherans (etc.), unbaptized, parents of child catechumens, and parents of children preparing for first Communion or confirmation.

Was it messy? You bet. In the same way Thanksgiving dinner is messy. But we all pitched in, and we had some amazing conversations. It was a compromise from the ideal, but it was clear to the baptized candidates that they were already members of a community of baptized believers. And we always kept before ourselves the goal of developing more catechists and providing more specialized catechetical processes in the future. In other words, we did not settle for the compromises as "just the way things are around here."

How to move to separate processes

Okay, so now you're convinced that you should have separate processes for the baptized candidates and the catechumens. But you currently have a combined process, and separating the two would be much too difficult right now. What do you do? Here are seven simple steps to move to separate processes.

1. *Change your initial interview.* From now on, whenever a baptized person comes to you to discuss becoming Catholic, use words like "receiving" him into the Catholic Church and talk about him "coming into full communion." Do not talk about "completing his initiation," "RCIA," "catechumenate," or "Easter Vigil."

2. ***Schedule the next Rite of Welcome on a different Sunday*** than the next Rite of Acceptance. If possible, schedule it at a different Mass time from the Rite of Acceptance.

3. ***Change the way you celebrate the Rite of Welcome.*** (See TeamRCIA. com for a ritual outline.) Deemphasize the elements that symbolize initial conversion. For example, do the rite inside the church and omit the signings.

4. ***Change the structure of your catechetical process.***

   a. If you have or can recruit enough volunteers, establish three different small groups for catechesis: the catechumens, the baptized-uncatechized, and the baptized-catechized.

   b. If you aren't able to maintain three separate groups, consider two groups: one for the catechumens and the baptized-uncatechized candidates and a second group for the baptized-catechized candidates. Remember the baptized-catechized candidates do not need a full catechetical process parallel to the catechumenate. What they do need would require a simple short-term commitment from a catechist.

If you already have adult formation groups for Catholics (e.g., Bible study, RENEW, parents whose children are preparing to celebrate sacraments, small Christian communities), you can place the baptized-catechized candidates into one of those groups. Some of the groups might need to make small adjustments in their agendas, and most would be happy to do so for a short while to help prepare someone for full communion.

   c. If you are not able to even manage two separate groups, consider expanding your single group to include some of the regular parishioners for their own ongoing formation. You might also include some of the parents whose children are preparing to celebrate sacraments. In this way, the candidates are formed with other baptized members of the parish. This can get messy, but as long as everyone understands it is temporary until you can develop more catechists, it can be a very rich experience.

5. ***Keep the baptized with the baptized at Mass.*** Only dismiss the catechumens. Some people argue that since those who are not yet in full communion can't receive Communion, it is more hospitable

to dismiss them. As well-intentioned as this is, it mis-catechizes the parish about the role of the baptismal priesthood in the liturgy. All of the baptized, even those in imperfect communion, exercise their baptismal priesthood in the praying of the general intercessions and in the offering of the sacrifice of praise in the Eucharistic Prayer. Participating in this priestly action teaches the baptized candidates what "full communion" looks like and catechizes the parishioners that the candidates are not simply "non-Catholics." They are brothers and sisters in Christ.

In most parishes on Sunday, there are others at Mass who are not able to receive Communion whom we would never consider dismissing. For example, most of our assemblies include children who have not yet received their first Communion, those who are conscious of serious sin, and other baptized people who are not in a process to become Catholic. The arguments about hospitable dismissal are not made for these people and ought not be made for the baptized candidates for full communion.

6. *Start doing the Rite of Reception at Sunday Mass.* This should be an easy call for the baptized-catechized. The RCIA is pretty clear that bringing these folks to full communion at the Easter Vigil could be percieved as triumphalism. (See National Statutes 32-33.) The Rite of Reception (487-498) is structurally very simple (although it is spiritually very profound). It doesn't take a lot of work to insert it into a Sunday liturgy, and it is short enough that it does not add a lot of time to the liturgy. (See TeamRCIA.com for a ritual outline.)

You might consider also celebrating the Rite of Reception at a Sunday Mass with the baptized-uncatechized candidates as well. The RCIA is more flexible about allowing these folks to be received into full communion at the Easter Vigil, however. But if you look at the section of the RCIA where the Easter Vigil reception of the already baptized is discussed (564), it reminds us that the decision to combine it with the sacraments of initiation must be guided by the norms listed at 475:2. So flip open your RCIA to that spot, and you will see the triumphalism concern again.

Any appearance of triumphalism should be carefully avoided....
Both the ecumenical implications and the bond between the

candidate and the parish community should be considered. Often it will be preferable to celebrate the Mass with only a few relatives and friends.

If the baptized-uncatechized candidate is a Catholic (someone baptized Catholic as an infant, but never raised to practice the faith), then the Easter Vigil is the appropriate place for them to celebrate confirmation and Eucharist. Catholics believe that that person's initiation remains incomplete, and the Vigil is the premier moment of initiation. And there can obviously be no fear of appearing triumphalistic and anti-ecumenical.

7. ***Discontinue celebrating the combined Rite of Sending and the Rite of Calling the Candidates to Continuing Conversion.*** Some dioceses do not celebrate a combined Rite of Election and Call to Continuing Conversion, so there is no reason to celebrate a Rite of Sending with the baptized candidates in those places. However, even if your diocese does celebrate a combined rite, there is no obligation for you to send the baptized candidates to the cathedral (as there is with the catechumens).

At the very least, you would not be celebrating these rites with the baptized, catechized candidates. Because they are catechized, their time of preparation is very short. They would be received into full communion as soon as they are ready, which is likely to be well before Lent when these combined rites are celebrated.

22

What about Catholics?

When Catholics come knocking, you're dealing with three different types of folks.

CATECHIZED

Catechized Catholics are those folks who missed confirmation and are now interested in "catching up." They're in church most Sundays, and they are regularly going to Communion. They need very little additional formation. If they are full and active participants in the Eucharist, how much more catechesis could they need to be confirmed? They absolutely should not be placed in the catechumenate process.

There may be cases in which a catechized Catholic also needs to celebrate first Communion, but these instances are less common. You would need to discern how much additional catechesis they would need in order to celebrate confirmation and first Communion, but they would not need a lengthy process parallel to the catechumenate.

UNCATECHIZED

These are the people who were baptized as infants but were never raised as Catholics. We can speak of these folks as never having completed their initiation. They can appropriately be placed in the catechumenate and complete their initiation at the Easter Vigil. They can also complete their initiation at one of the Masses during the Easter season.

You may also encounter Catholics who celebrated their first Communion around age seven and haven't been back to church since. Strictly speaking, these folks are catechized because they would have had to have been in order to celebrate first Communion. You will have to do some discernment to determine the best course for them. It might be appropriate to place them in the catechumenate, but they may not need a full liturgical year before they are sufficiently catechized to celebrate confirmation.

RETURNING CATHOLICS

These are folks who have been fully initiated but have been absent from the church for some time and have not been living the Catholic life. We can think of these folks as returning to or recovering their baptismal commitment. However, their issues and struggles are likely to be quite different from the catechumens and the uncatechized Catholics. If you have the resources available, the ideal situation would be to form a separate formation group for returning Catholics. But be sure you assign them strong companions whom they can lean on and with whom they can develop a trust relationship.

23

The Catechumens at Home

There is a persistent difficulty in most parishes that needs to be addressed in the catechumenate. That is, most parishes think of "church" as the big building with its steeple and parking lot.

What if instead of thinking of church as a place we went to, we thought of it as an activity we did? Where is church *done*? Where does it *happen*?

Can you stand another analogy? Maybe a way to think about this is like cooking. Where do we cook? I do a lot of cooking, and I do it mostly at home. But I live in a small condo. When I want to cook for a crowd, I have to go somewhere else to do it. And if I want to learn how to be a better cook, there are places I can go to do that. If I want to discuss cooking with other cooks, there's a place for that as well. And what if I wanted to teach others to cook? Well, I could certainly teach people right in my own kitchen (and I have!). And I could also gather a larger group and have more formal classes at a restaurant or a cooking school. (I'm not *that* good; it's just an example.)

So what if we thought of church that way? Church is an activity, a mission of spreading the good news, learning how to do that better, teaching others how to do it. And most of it happens at home. I didn't just think this up. It is an idea that was central at the Second Vatican Council. In the Constitution on the Church, the council said:

> The family is, so to speak, the domestic church. In it parents should, by their word and example, be the first preachers of the faith to their children…. (11)

157

The *General Directory for Catechesis* expands on that central idea:

> The family is defined as a "domestic Church," that is, in every Christian family the different aspects and functions of the life of the entire Church may be reflected: mission; catechesis; witness; prayer, etc. Indeed in the same way as the Church, the family "is a place in which the Gospel is transmitted and from which it extends." [*Evangelii Nuntiandi*, 71]
>
> The family as a *locus* of catechesis has a unique privilege: transmitting the Gospel by rooting it in the context of profound human values. On this human base, Christian initiation is more profound: the awakening of the sense of God; the first steps in prayer; education of the moral conscience; formation in the Christian sense of human love, understood as a reflection of the love of God the Father, the Creator. (255)

 "Family" does not mean only the stereotypical two-parent household with 2.5 children, a dog, and a couple of goldfish. It is any domestic situation where Christians are living and doing church.

This is quite an agenda for the families of the catechumens! And it might change our job description as catechumenate leaders. If we think of our job as providing resources for the catechists and the catechumens, we have to add to that providing resources for the domestic churches where the catechumens live.

This isn't necessarily a lot more work. If you have an active parish school or religious education program, they are probably sending home spiritual resources and activities with the children. Ask if you can get copies of everything that goes home, and send it home with your catechumens as well. You might have to adapt it for adults. But if the catechumens have children (or if the catechumens *are* children), you might be able to use the materials as is.

In his book *Whole Community Catechesis in Plain English* (Twenty-Third Publications), Bill Huebsch recommends several activities that can help the domestic churches fulfill their catechetical mandate. Two in particular might be useful for the catechumens.

BREAKING OPEN THE WORD

Think of yourself as a resource center for the catechumenate families—like the dean of a cooking school. What is it they are going to need in order to cook up some church life in their homes? Just as every cook needs a chef's knife, every follower of Christ needs the word of God. Be sure that every catechumenate household has a Bible and a list of the Sunday readings. As part of their weekly faith practice, ask the catechumens to break open the word with their families.

 If you have a catechumen who lives alone, get creative. She can meet with her sponsor or another parishioner in her home. She can find an online community to meet with. She can journal about her reflections and share excerpts with a friend at a later time.

Huebsch suggests providing the catechumens, indeed the entire parish, with a question of the week that everyone focuses on. (See tinyurl.com/yrx8ej for some of his examples.)

If you aren't able to provide a weekly question, adapt the process I describe in Appendix 4 on how to lead a dismissal session. Encourage the catechumens to focus particularly on the "so what" section.

Specifically, after having prayerfully read the Sunday readings, have the family members ask how their lives might be different in the coming week. Have them tell each other what they have discovered about themselves, about each other, about God, or about the church.

Be sure they begin and end their breaking open the word with the sign of the cross and a prayer. You may need to write out a brief outline for them if the family is new to praying. For example:

> *The leader lights a candle. All make the sign of the cross.*
>
> **Leader:** Lord our God, we have gathered to share our faith in you. Open our ears as we listen to your word.
>
> *The leader or another member of the household reads the Sunday gospel.*
>
> **Leader:** Let's all share a little bit about what we *saw* in the reading.
>
> *All share.*

Leader: Let's all share a little bit about what we *heard* in the reading.

All share.

Leader: Let's all share a little bit about what the reading means and how we might live differently as a family because of its message.

All share.

Leader: Let us now gather all these thoughts and offer them to God in the prayer that Jesus taught us.

All pray the Lord's Prayer. Conclude with the sign of the cross.

If your parish uses a question of the week, the leader could ask that question instead of these. If the family is familiar with praying together, they could also incorporate their own spontaneous prayers at the end before the Lord's Prayer.

50-50 CONTRACT

Another terrific idea Huebsch suggests is developing a 50-50 faith formation contract between the parish and parish households. He makes the point that parish households are *already* living a life of faith. This must certainly be true in the homes of the catechumens or else how would they have come to their initial faith? So we don't have to do any *programming*. We just have to affirm what is already happening.

In a 50-50 plan the households make a formal promise to live the Christian life and to support each other in that life. They promise to take on a teaching role to hand on their faith to those in the household who are growing in the Spirit.

Likewise, the parish staff and community make a formal promise. They agree to provide excellent worship, formation, community, and public witness. And they agree to provide a wealth of resources to the parish households to assist them on their journey of faith.

Huebsch says moving to an agreement like this "provides us a chance to 'start over' on new ground in how we provide catechesis. The new ground is that no matter what, catechesis is always done on a 50-50 Plan, household and parish. It's never the duty of just one or the other" (*Whole Community Catechesis in Plain English*, 63; for an example agreement, see pages 60-63 of his book).

24 Prepare to Initiate

When I was younger and much more naïve, I believed that if all our parishes seriously engaged in the catechumenate—if we put our heart and soul into it—we could change the world. I still believe that. It's just taking a little longer than I first hoped.

At the beginning of this book, I suggested that the delay might be due to us having gotten into a comfort zone with our initiation ministries. I wondered if we might be a little burnt out, thinking about how much energy we have expended and how much we have accomplished with so few resources. Maybe we're all taking a well-deserved breather and saying to ourselves, "We've done pretty good." And I suggested that a little rest is fine. But if we settle for pretty good, or good enough, we will never fully accomplish the mission Jesus charged us with—to go and baptize.

I went on to say that while developing an excellent catechumenate process does take a lot of work, it is not beyond our talents. God has given us all the gifts we need to accomplish so great a mission. There are two gifts in particular that are required: humility and passion.

I know you have those gifts, or you would not be in this ministry. And I know one other thing. There is no better person than you to be a leader in initiation ministry in your community. There will be others with different gifts, perhaps with gifts you do not have. But no one has what you have—your unique faith journey that has led you to this exact place in your life and in the life of your community.

In other words, if you're looking for the right person to come along who has the skills and charisma and authority and whatever else you think is missing to move your community to an excellent catechumenate process—rub some Windex on your bathroom mirror.

But I hope I've made it clear that it's not *all* up to you. What is up to you *is up to you*. Whatever your call and whatever your unique role in the ministry of initiation, do it with humility and passion.

I've written this book to help you do that. I trust that you are now going to use those singular talents God has given you to move your community from doing a good RCIA to engaging in an excellent catechumenate process.

If I can help, e-mail me at Nick@TeamRCIA.com. And don't worry. You're going to be great.

Glossary

Inquirer A person seeking basic information about Catholicism or Christianity. This person may or may not eventually join the church. Also called a "precatechumen."

Catechumen An unbaptized person who is preparing for full initiation at the Easter Vigil.

Convert Another term for a catechumen. "Convert" should never be used to refer to a baptized person who is preparing to become a Catholic.

Candidate A baptized Christian who is preparing to become a Catholic. In the *Rite of Christian Initiation of Adults*, the term is also used to refer to the subjects of a rite, which may include catechumens, inquirers, and baptized Christians.

Catechumenate The period of time and the structure within which the catechumens prepare for initiation. "Catechumenate" is also used as a synonym for the entire *Rite of Christian Initiation of Adults*.

Elect Catechumens who have gone through the Rite of Election or Enrollment Rite. The Elect are those who are involved in immediate preparation for initiation at the upcoming Easter Vigil.

Sponsor A companion who walks with a catechumen or candidate through the catechumenate process. Ideally assigned by the parish, in discussion with the catechumen or candidate.

Godparent Someone who makes a lifelong commitment to be a spiritual mentor to a catechumen who decides to be baptized. Chosen by the catechumen. Possibly the same person as the sponsor.

Triduum The "three days" of Easter. *Day 1:* Holy Thursday evening to Good Friday evening. *Day 2:* Good Friday evening to Holy Saturday evening. *Day 3:* Easter Vigil to Easter Sunday Evening Prayer.

Neophyte A newly baptized person.

RCIC and **RCIY** Fictional beasts. There is only one rite—the *Rite of Christian Initiation of Adults.* Adaptations of this one rite are made for children, youth, and previously baptized people. The only appropriate acronym is "RCIA." In the parish, more user-friendly terms are encouraged.

Moving to a Year-Round Model

What if you have already started your catechumenate process and you have a nine-month model? How do you move to a year-round process?

It feels like it would be difficult because, well, you'd have to work *all year round*. I'm not going to tell you it's not more work. But it's not as much work as you might think. The hardest part of the shift is simply imagining things *can* shift. Once you imagine it, the rest of the work is relatively easy.

Let's imagine it's late October in your parish and you celebrated the Rite of Acceptance two weeks ago. Someone has just called the parish asking about becoming Catholic. What do you do?

Do you invite him to the next catechumenate session, assign him a sponsor, and meet with him privately to catch him up with the rest of the group? And what if you get two or three more like that before Easter? Do you try to do the same thing with them?

Or do you tell these inquirers that the catechumenate is "closed" for this year, and they will have to wait until August (or whenever you start) to begin with the next "precatechumenate class"?

Let me suggest a third way. If anyone shows up in the next week or the next month or anytime before the Easter Vigil asking questions about becoming Catholic, invite them to meet with your ambassador of welcome (precatechumenate coordinator; see chapter 15). If you don't have an ambassador of welcome, put that at the very top of your to-do list.

Set up a meeting within a few days of your initial encounter. Make sure your ambassador of welcome has significant contact with the inquirer at least once a month until it is time for your next Rite of Acceptance. (Significant is at least forty-five minutes.)

The monthly meeting doesn't have to be "catechesis." In fact, it's not supposed to be. Let's say the first meeting is at a coffee shop or a restaurant, and the ambassador of welcome has one task: to get to know the inquirer. Where does he come from? What is his family like? What kind of work does he do? What kind of hobbies does he have? Why is he interested in Catholicism?

The next monthly meeting might be the parish day to decorate the church for Christmas. Or it might be helping with the holiday food drive. What is it your parish is doing that month, and how can your ambassador of welcome involve the inquirers?

Now it's January. One or two more inquirers have shown up. Gather them all, with their spouses and children if they have families, at a parishioner's house for an evening of cookies and hot chocolate. Ask them to tell you stories about times when they've noticed God in their lives. And you tell them stories about when you've noticed God in your life.

In February, ask them if they'd like to observe the Ash Wednesday liturgy. Invite them out for coffee after the liturgy to share their reactions. Ask them what they thought of the prayer. Ask them if they ever pray. Maybe they'd like to say a short prayer with you before you all depart.

And so on. The point is, find creative ways to let the work of the parish assist you in evangelizing the inquirers and drawing them more deeply into the life of faith. Continue meeting with them in these creative, monthly ways until your usual precatechumenate sessions start. If you make that your normative practice, you will have moved to a year-round pre-catechumenate. The only extra work is finding someone who is willing to gather the inquirers once a month for a creative activity or meeting.

Once you've moved to a continuous precatechumentate, it is relatively simple to move to a continuous catechumenate. For more ideas, visit TeamRCIA.com.

Rehearsal Outlines

REHEARSAL OUTLINE: RITE OF ACCEPTANCE (RCIA 48-68)

(This schedule assumes it is still light enough at the beginning of rehearsal to read outdoors. If that is not the case, adjust the rehearsal time or provide light.)

6:30 Before everyone arrives turn on lights and set up microphones; put the lectionary or Book of Gospels on the ambo; put the presider's script or ritual book on his chair; put the catechumenate director's script on her chair or pew; place name tags in the pews where you want the catechumens and their sponsors to sit.

If necessary, mark the spots in the aisles where the catechumens will stand with a piece of masking tape.

7:00 Welcome the participants: the presider, the director of the catechumenate, the sponsors, an acolyte to hold the presider's book, a cross bearer, perhaps a hospitality minister, and perhaps the musician. (The inquirers are not present.) Ask the presider, sponsors, acolyte, and catechumenate director to sit in their places. Lead a brief prayer.

7:05 Remind the sponsors of these essential points; be lighthearted, but still convey the importance of the information:

- Point out to the sponsors that this rite has two primary elements—the embrace of the cross and the gospel way of life and the crossing over the threshold.

- Sponsors need to pick up their inquirers from home or meet them in front of the church before Mass.

- The sponsors and inquirers remain outside the church; the assembly will be processing out to greet them. They need to stand with their candidates at the places you will show them in a minute.

- From the minute they meet their inquirer on Sunday, until the minute the new catechumens are dismissed, the sponsors need to be in physical contact. A hand on an arm or shoulder at all times.
- It is the sponsors' responsibility to know the details of the rite. They need to project an air of confidence and always reassure the inquirer that things are under control.

7:15 *Receiving the candidates:* Ask the cross bearer to retrieve the cross and lead everyone outside. Remind the sponsors they will already be outside.

♫ *Ask the musician to prepare an appropriate processional song that can be sung without books.*

If you have a hospitality minister, ask her to stay close to the cross bearer and open the doors.

Greeting: The rite presumes the presider is greeting the candidates. If he is unfamiliar with them or with the rite, the director of the catechumenate might also greet them. Whoever greets, it should be warm and inviting. No text is given in the rite, so you may need to compose something. Ask the presider to rehearse it now.

Opening dialogue: This should flow directly from the greeting and should not seem like an additional part of the liturgy. Adapt the text in the rite to have the presider speak to the sponsors. He should ask the sponsors to introduce their companions to the assembly. Ask the sponsors to practice what they will say. Remind them to speak loudly so everyone outside can hear. Go through each one. Once all are introduced, he asks each inquirer individually, *"N., what do you ask of God's church?"*

Ask the sponsors (or a proxy for the candidates if you have other team members at the rehearsal) to answer something (anything) as though they were the inquirer for the sake of rehearsal. If you have prepared the inquirers as suggested in chapter 10, they will not likely answer, "Faith." The presider will need to remember what each person asks for and respond, *"N., what does [what the inquirer said] offer you?"*

Alert the sponsors to remember the inquirers' answers. They will need to repeat them later in the rite.

7:25 *Candidates' first Acceptance of the Gospel:* Remember this is not the acceptance of the Book of Gospels or a Bible, but rather the gospel way of life. At this point the cross bearer gives the cross to the presider who then stands with it directly in front the first inquirer.

The sponsor or the presider assists the inquirer in wrapping his hands around the cross, and the presider covers the inquirer's hands with his own. Recalling what the inquirer asked for, the presider says, *"N., this is [what the inquirer said]."*

He then continues spontaneously, using one of the three texts at paragraph 52 as a model. If your presider is not good at speaking spontaneously or if he is unfamiliar with the rite, put option C in his script. However, change the phrase, "This is eternal life" to "This is _____". The presider will fill in the blank with whatever the inquirer asked for and then continue on with the text as written.

Have him rehearse this now, using the answers given by the inquirer stand-ins for practice.

♫ *There can be a sung acclamation after each inquirer accepts the teachings of the gospel.*

7:35 *Affirmation by the sponsors and the assembly:* Have the presider ask for the affirmation as given at paragraph 53.

Signing of the candidates with the cross: Decide before rehearsal if you are going to sign the candidates only on the forehead or sign all their senses (see paragraph 56).

Also decide beforehand if the presider is going to physically sign each candidate or if he will make a sign of the cross over all of them together.

Speak to the sponsors now, and convey these points:

- They should still have their hand on their candidates.
- After the presider signs the candidates (either one by one or all together), they turn to face their candidates, keeping a hand on them.
- They then make the sign of the cross on their candidate's forehead.
- They do this with an open palm, *not a thumb.*
- They apply some pressure so the candidate *feels* the cross.
- As the presider calls out each of the other senses, the sponsors press an open-palm sign of the cross into each sense named. Have them practice this action on each other, going through each sign.
- For the final signing, the sponsors, along with the presider, make a large sign of the cross over the candidates' whole body (without touching them).
- Point out that from this point on, the candidates are catechumens.

♫ *Ideally, there is a sung acclamation after each declaration of the sense to be signed. The sponsors do the actual signing as the acclamation is sung.*

Concluding prayer: Choose before rehearsal option A or B at paragraph 57.

♫ *The concluding prayer could be sung by the presider.*

Invitation to the celebration of the Word of God: Have the presider read the line at paragraph 60. The procession is led by the cross, followed by the catechumens and their sponsors, followed by the presider, followed by the rest of the assembly.

Once inside the church, have the sponsors sit where you have reserved spaces for them.

The Liturgy of the Word

7:45 *Presentation of a Bible:* Decide before the rehearsal if you are going to include this optional part of the rite. Decide also if you are going to adapt it to be a presentation of the Book of Gospels. (See chapter 9.) If you are including the rite, tell the sponsors these details:

- Remind them that they need to remember what their catechumens previously asked from the church at the beginning of the liturgy and what that offers them.
- After the homily, the presider will ask the catechumens to please stand.
- The sponsors will then lead their catechumens to the spots you've designated. (Have them go there now.)
- Remind them to keep a hand on their catechumens.
- The director of the catechumenate or another minister goes to the ambo to get the Book of Gospels, or she retrieves the Bibles. (Have her go there now.)
- The director will then present the (open) Book of Gospels or a Bible to each catechumen.

Ask the director to walk to the first catechumen and stand there as though the catechumen were in front of her.

The director then says to the catechumen, "N., receive the Gospel of Jesus Christ."

Now have the sponsor mime taking the catechumen's hand and placing it on the book. (Alternatively, you could have the catechumens kiss the book after the following dialogue).

At this point, the sponsor speaks to the catechumen by name, recalling what he asked for and offering a hope that what he seeks will be found in the Word. For example, "N., this Gospel offers *[peace]* that surpasses all understanding. May you find in it *[a community of love]* to support you on your journey."

Remind the sponsors they won't know exactly what to say until the day of the ritual when they hear what their candidates ask for.

Ask the director to go to each position, and have each sponsor practice.

♫ *The assembly can sing an acclamation as the director processes from catechumen to catechumen.*

7:55 Intercessions: Explain that the intercessions and the prayer over the catechumens will be prayed at this point. (There is no need to actually read through them.) Tell the sponsors that they remain at their places with their catechumen during the intercessions.

Point out to the sponsors that these are intercessions *for* the catechumens and not the prayer of the faithful that we usually do at Mass.

(Remind them to keep a hand on their catechumen.)

♫ *The intercessions could be chanted.*

Dismissal: The presider reads the dismissal line. (Write one or choose one of the options in the ritual text before rehearsal.)

The director of the catechumenate exits down the main aisle, carrying the Book of Gospels or the lectionary.

Tell the sponsors to tell the catechumens at that point to follow the book. Remind them that the catechumens might be momentarily confused. The sponsors should make sure the catechumens know what to do.

After the catechumens have left, the sponsors will return to their pews.

♫ *There would ordinarily be an acclamation as the catechumens leave.*

8:00 End: Thank the sponsors for their time and their commitment. Remind them to be in front of the church 15 minutes early. Make sure they have your e-mail address and cell phone number in case they have any questions.

REHEARSAL OUTLINE: SENDING OF THE CATECHUMENS FOR ELECTION (RCIA 106-117)

6:30 Before everyone arrives turn on lights and put out microphones; put a stand or table for the Book of the Elect in place; place the book and a substantial pen on it; put the lectionary on the ambo; set up a microphone for the testimonies if necessary; put the presider's script or ritual book on his chair; put the catechumenate director's script on her chair or pew; place name tags in the pews where you want the catechumens and their godparents to sit.

If necessary, mark the spots in the aisles where the catechumens will stand with a piece of masking tape.

7:00 Welcome the participants: the presider, the director of the catechumenate, the godparents, and perhaps the musician. (The catechumens are not present.) Ask the presider, godparents, and catechumenate director to sit in their places. Lead a brief prayer.

7:10 Remind the godparents of these essential points; be lighthearted, but still convey the importance of the information:

- Point out to the godparents that this rite has two primary elements— the testimony of the godparents (and the assembly) and the signing of the Book of the Elect

- Godparents need to pick up their catechumens from home or meet them in front of the church before Mass.

- Everyone needs to be in their seats 15 minutes before Mass starts.

- From the minute they walk into the church, until the minute the catechumens are dismissed, the godparents need to be in physical contact with their catechumens—hand on an arm or shoulder at all times.

- It is the godparents' responsibility to know the details of the rite. They need to project an air of confidence and always reassure the catechumens that things are under control.

- Point out to them that Mass will begin as usual and will be "normal" up through the homily. After the homily ends, they need to be ready.

7:20 *Presentation of the candidates:* The catechumenate director moves to her microphone and reads her lines at paragraph 111 in the RCIA. (Remember, these lines can be adapted, but you need to do that before rehearsal.)

The presider calls forth the catechumens. He can make a general call (paragraph 111) followed by the name of each catechumen. Or he can make a general call, and the director of the catechumenate calls each individual name.

When the godparent hears his catechumen's name, he mimes taking the catechumen by the arm and walking the catechumen to the spot you have chosen.

♫ *The cantor could chant the names of the catechumens to call them forward.*

7:25 *Affirmation by the godparents:* The presider reads his lines (paragraph 112). Decide beforehand if the godparents are going to give extended testimony, and adapt the presider's lines accordingly and plan to work with the godparents on preparing their testimony (see chapter 11). If the godparents will be giving extended testimony, instruct them about these things:

- The order in which they will testify. (They don't need to go in any particular order, but then tell them that also.)
- They need to speak loudly, even if they have a microphone. (Practice a few lines to see how they sound.)
- If you or another member of the team will be working with them on their testimony at a later time, tell them when and where to meet.

If you will not be doing extended testimony, have the presider read through the questions and have the godparents respond. Make sure they respond loudly and clearly.

(Remind them to keep a hand on their catechumen.)

♫ *There can be a sung acclamation after the testimonies. If you are doing extended testimonies, perhaps there is an acclamation after every three or so.*

7:35 *Affirmation by the assembly:* Have the presider ask for the assembly's affirmation. This can also be an extended testimony by the assembly if you have time. Or it can be a simple question to which the assembly responds "Yes" or "We do." However, there is no question in the ritual text. You will need to write one.

7:40 *Signing of the book:* (If the signing is to take place in the presence of the bishop later at the Rite of Election, you omit it in the parish Rite of Sending; RCIA, 113.) The presider concludes the affirmations with a call to the catechumens to sign the book. You will need to write this invitation; it is not in the ritual text.

The godparents act out escorting their catechumens to the book and handing them the pen to sign with. Tell them what order to go in and how long to wait between signings. Tell them to return to their marked spot after their catechumen has signed. Walk it through with each godparent. (The godparents would not ordinarily sign the book.)

(Remind them to keep a hand on their catechumen.)

Point out to the godparents that even though the catechumens will have signed the Book of the Elect, they will not *be* elect until the bishop declares them to be elected at the Rite of Election.

♪ *There can be a sung acclamation after each signing. There should be a more extended acclamation after all the signings. You or the director or the presider could process the Book of the Elect (open) through the assembly at this point.*

7:50 *Intercessions:* The intercessions and the prayer over the catechumens will be prayed at this point. (There is no need to actually read through them.)

Point out to the godparents that these are intercessions *for* the catechumens and not the prayer of the faithful that we usually do at Mass.

(Remind them to keep a hand on their catechumen.)

♪ *The intercessions could be chanted.*

Dismissal: The presider reads the dismissal line. (Write one or choose one of the options in the ritual text before rehearsal.)

The director of the catechumenate exits down the main aisle, carrying the Book of the Gospels or the lectionary.

Tell the godparents to tell the catechumens to follow the book. Remind them that even though the catechumens will be used to a dismissal, the flow of the liturgy will be new to them and they might be momentarily confused. The godparents should make sure the catechumens know what to do.

After the catechumens have left, the godparents will return to their pews.

♪ *There would ordinarily be an acclamation as the catechumens leave.*

8:00 *End:* Thank the godparents for their time and their commitment. Remind them to be in their seats 15 minutes early. Make sure they have your e-mail address and cell phone number in case they have any questions.

REHEARSAL OUTLINE: SCRUTINY
(RCIA 150-156, 164-170, 171-177)

6:30 Before everyone arrives turn on lights and put out microphones; put the lectionary on the ambo; put the presider's script or ritual book on his chair; put the catechumenate director's script on her chair or pew; place name tags in the pews where you want the elect and their godparents to sit.

If necessary, mark the spots in the aisles where the elect will stand with a piece of masking tape.

7:00 Welcome the participants: the presider, the director of the catechumenate, the godparents, an acolyte to hold the presider's book, and perhaps the musician. (The elect are not present.) Ask the presider, godparents, acolyte, and catechumenate director to sit in their places. Lead a brief prayer.

7:10 Remind the godparents of these essential points; be lighthearted, but still convey the importance of the information:

- Point out to the godparents that the scrutinies have two goals—to uncover and heal all weakness in the elect; to strengthen all that is strong and good in the elect (see RCIA 141).

- There are three scrutinies, and all three are required because one builds upon the next. (There only needs to be one rehearsal, however.)

- Godparents need to pick up the elect from home or meet them in front of the church before Mass.

- Everyone needs to be in their seats 15 minutes before Mass starts.

- From the minute they walk into the church, until the minute the elect are dismissed, the godparents need to be in physical contact with the elect. A hand on an arm or shoulder at all times.

- It is the godparents' responsibility to know the details of the rite. They need to project an air of confidence and always reassure the elect that things are under control.

- Point out to them that Mass will begin as usual and will be "normal" up through the homily. After the homily ends, they need to be ready.

7:20 Invitation to silent prayer: After the homily, the godparents move the elect into place. There is no cue for them in the ritual text. You can write one for the presider to say, but do that before rehearsal. Have them mime bringing the elect to their spots.

The presider first invites the assembly to stand and pray. (The rite has the assembly stand *after* the silent prayer, but it makes more sense to have them stand here.) No text is given. The presider can improvise, or you can prepare a script ahead of time. In either case, have him say his lines now.

The presider then invites the elect to pray. Decide ahead of time if the elect are going to bow their heads or kneel. Have the presider read the line in the ritual text.

7:30 Intercessions for the elect: Note that the intercessions for the elect will be prayed at this point. (There is no need to actually read through them.) The rite has the elect standing at this point, but, if they knelt for the silent prayer, it might be more appropriate for them to remain kneeling as the community prays for them. Decide this ahead of time. (See chapter 12.) (If they will kneel for the intercessions, decide if cushions are necessary.)

Point out to the godparents that these are intercessions *for* the elect and not the prayer of the faithful that we usually do at Mass.

(Remind them to keep a hand on the elect.)

♫ *The intercessions could be chanted.*

7:35 Exorcism: Point out to the godparents that the exorcism will follow. Explain to them that this isn't the kind of exorcism they may have seen in movies. It is a simple but profound prayer that the elect will be freed from the power of sin and temptation.

Have the presider practice the first part of the exorcism prayer with hands joined. Then have him go to each place where the elect will be and mime laying hands on their heads. If you are adapting the rite as suggested in chapter 12, then the director of the catechumenate follows and likewise mimes the laying on of hands.

After the director has moved to the next place, the godparent steps in front of her elect and lays hands on the head of the elect. Walk through the entire laying on of hands.

♫ *The laying on of hands is always done in silence.*

The presider and the director return to their places, and the godparents return to standing next to the elect, hands on shoulders.

In the liturgy, the presider prays the conclusion of the exorcism with his arms outstretched. Have him practice now.

If the elect are still kneeling, they would stand after the "Amen." Tell the godparents they will need to remember that and help the elect to their feet.

7:45 Dismissal: The presider reads the dismissal line. (Write one or choose one of the options in the ritual text before rehearsal.)

The director of the catechumenate exits down the main aisle, carrying the Book of Gospels or the lectionary.

Tell the godparents to tell the elect to follow the book. Remind them that even though the elect will be used to a dismissal, the flow of the liturgy will be new to them and they might be momentarily confused. The godparents should make sure the elect know what to do.

After the elect have left, the godparents will return to their pews.

♫ *There would ordinarily be an acclamation as the elect and any other catechumens leave.*

7:50 End: Thank the godparents for their time and their commitment. Remind them to be in their seats fifteen minutes early. Make sure they have your e-mail address and cell phone number in case they have any questions.

Dismissal and Catechetical Session Outlines

HOW TO LEAD A 30-MINUTE DISMISSAL SESSION

The basics are not too difficult. There are three things to pay attention to:

1. The room
2. The flow of the faith sharing
3. The "so what"

THE ROOM

When you leave the Mass with the catechumens, you need to go somewhere. (Traditionally, this room is called a *catechumeneon*.) Make sure the room is prepared ahead of time. The faith sharing after dismissal is not catechesis. It is an extension of the liturgy. So, if possible, you want to go to a room other than a classroom or the catechetical space. If that's not possible, try to make the catechetical space look more like a prayer room and less like a classroom. You might want to have a candle, a cross, some flowers, and possibly a stand for the Book of Gospels or the lectionary.

Have the chairs arranged in a circle, and place a Bible on each chair.

THE FLOW

1 minute: Try to maintain an attitude of prayer as you gather. There will be time for socializing later. A simple way to keep the prayerful sense of the liturgy is to recite the verse of the responsorial psalm from Mass and have the catechumens recite it back. If you are at all musical, by all means, sing it.

8 minutes: Next have everyone sit in the circle. Begin the faith sharing with a statement like this:

Today we heard readings from _____, _____, and _____. What do you remember most from the Gospel reading?

Encourage everyone to share something they remembered.

What do you see?

8 minutes: After everyone has spoken, ask them to go deeper into the reading. Have them open their Bibles to the passage. Ask them each to name something they *see* in the reading. Keep going deeper, and keep focused on what they see. Characters, scenery, actions, crowds. Ask them to describe things in as much details as they can.

What do you hear?

Now go around again, asking everyone what they *hear* in the reading. Background sounds, quietness, wind, people talking. Pay particular attention to questions they hear spoken. Ask them if they heard anything new or surprising.

So what?

8 minutes: Ask everyone to reflect in silence for a minute on why they think these readings matter. After some silence, ask the group questions about what the readings mean. If your parish uses a question of the week, focus on that. Or ask how, having seen and heard what they have, their lives might be different in the coming week. Ask if they have discovered anything new about themselves, about God, or about the church. Ask what questions they are struggling with.

5 minutes: Summarize what you heard from the group. Close with a prayer of your own or the Lord's Prayer and the sign of the cross.

HOW TO LEAD A 90-MINUTE CATECHETICAL SESSION
Preparation

1. Prayerfully **read the Scriptures** for Sunday

2. **Read a commentary** on the Scriptures

3. Identify at least **three church teachings** that flow from the readings (you won't use all three, but it helps to be prepared)

4. Look up related topics in the **Catechism of the Catholic Church** to refresh your understanding of these teachings

5. For each of the three church teachings, make a list of at least *six points that you want to emphasize* for the catechumens. You'll have a list of at least 18 points related to church teaching (you won't use more than a few, but you don't know which ones you'll need). So your outline might look like this:

TEACHING 1	TEACHING 2	TEACHING 3
Subpoint	Subpoint	Subpoint
Subpoint	Subpoint	Subpoint
Subpoint	Subpoint	Subpoint
Subpoint	Subpoint	Subpoint
Subpoint	Subpoint	Subpoint
Subpoint	Subpoint	Subpoint

Catechetical session

(This can take place on Sunday after the conclusion of Mass or later during the week.)

10 MINUTES: GATHERING

1. Greet everyone as they arrive. Invite them to sit in a circle. Provide Bibles to those who did not bring one.

2. Lead the group in prayer.

3. If you are meeting right after Mass, ask someone to read the gospel from Mass.

4. If you are meeting later in the week, lead the group in a guided meditation, walking briefly, but prayerfully, through the Sunday liturgy.

30 MINUTES: MYSTAGOGICAL REFLECTION

1. Ask the catechumens to review for the group some of the points they discussed in their dismissal session.

2. As they speak make a mental note of which points connect with your list of church teaching points you want to emphasize.

3. As they speak, listen for places where they seem most energized.

4. Invite the sponsors to share their understandings of the readings, particularly the points raised by the catechumens.

5. Ask open-ended questions to explore the readings more deeply and lead the catechumens into a discussion of church teaching. For example:

- Why would Jesus do (say) that?
- How do you think the disciples reacted to that?
- If you were in Mark's (Matthew's, Luke's, John's) community in the first century and heard this story, how would you react?
- Why do you think the church still tells this story today?
- How is it possible for this story to have meaning for modern society?

10 MINUTES: BREAK

20 MINUTES: TEACHING

1. Based on the discussion, choose one of your major church teachings and three of the subpoints.

2. Discuss these three points with the catechumens. (The exact number of points you discuss is not important. What is important is not to overwhelm the catechumens. Over the course of the liturgical year, you'll have plenty of time to cover the basics of church teaching. You don't need to cram.)

3. If nothing the catechumens brought up in their discussion of the readings relates to what you prepared, you have two options:
   a. Do your best to discuss a church teaching that does relate to what they discussed. You won't be as well prepared, but it will be more meaningful to the catechumens. You can draw on the sponsors for help.
   b. Discuss something you have prepared anyway. Explain to the catechumens that this material also relates to the readings, and you had done your best to anticipate what they might want to discuss.

15 MINUTES: FAITH INTO ACTION

1. Go around the circle and ask each catechumen and sponsor:
   - what they learned about Jesus in the liturgy this week, and
   - how they will live differently this week based on what they learned from the liturgy.

2. Be sure to share your own learning and commitment to living in a new way.

5 MINUTES: CLOSE WITH PRAYER

Sundays with Appropriate Readings for the Rite of Acceptance

CYCLE A

Third Sunday in Ordinary Time

Is 8:23—9:3 • Ps 27:1, 4, 13–14 (1a) • 1 Cor 1:10–13, 17 • Mt 4:12–23

As he was walking by the Sea of Galilee, he saw two brothers, Simon who is called Peter, and his brother Andrew, casting a net into the sea; they were fishermen. He said to them, "Come after me, and I will make you fishers of men."

Fifth Sunday in Ordinary Time

Is 58:7–10 • Ps 112:4–5, 6–7, 8–9 • 1 Cor 2:1–5 • Mt 5:13–16

Your light must shine before others, that they may see your good deeds and glorify your heavenly Father.

Fourth Sunday of Easter

Acts 2:14a, 36–41 • Ps 23:1–3a, 3b–4, 5, 6 (1) • 1 Pt 2:20b–25 • Jn 10:1–10

Whoever enters by me will be saved, and will come in and go out and find pasture. The thief comes only to steal and kill and destroy. I came that they may have life, and have it abundantly.

Fifth Sunday of Easter

Acts 6:1–7 • Ps 33:1–2, 4–5, 18–19 (22) • 1 Pt 2:4–9 • Jn 14:1–12

Very truly, I tell you, the one who believes in me will also do the works that I do and, in fact, will do greater works than these, because I am going to the Father.

Sixth Sunday of Easter

Acts 8:5–8, 14–17 • Ps 66:1–3, 4–5, 6–7, 16, 20 • 1 Pt 3:15–18 • Jn 14:15–21

Those who love me will be loved by my Father, and I will love them and reveal myself to them.

Tenth Sunday in Ordinary Time

Hos 6:3–6 • Ps 50:1, 8, 12–13, 14–15 • Rom 4:18–25 • Mt 9:9–13

As Jesus was walking along, he saw a man called Matthew sitting at the tax booth; and he said to him, "Follow me." And he got up and followed him.

Twelfth Sunday in Ordinary Time

Jer 20:10–13 • Ps 69:8–10, 14, 17, 33–35 • Rom 5:12–15 • Mt 10:26–33

Everyone therefore who acknowledges me before others, I also will acknowledge before my Father in heaven; but whoever denies me before others, I also will deny before my Father in heaven.

Seventeenth Sunday in Ordinary Time

1 Kgs 3:5, 7–12 • Ps 119:57, 72, 76–77, 127–128, 129–130 • Rom 8:28–30 • Mt 13:44–52 or 13:44–46

The kingdom of heaven is like a merchant in search of fine pearls; on finding one pearl of great value, he went and sold all that he had and bought it.

Twenty-Second Sunday in Ordinary Time

Jer 20:7–9 • Ps 63:2, 3–4, 5–6, 8–9 (2b) • Rom 12:1–2 • Mt 16:21–27

Then Jesus told his disciples, "If any want to become my followers, let them deny themselves and take up their cross and follow me. For those who want to save their life will lose it, and those who lose their life for my sake will find it."

Thirty-First Sunday in Ordinary Time

Mal 1:14b—2:2b, 8–10 • Ps 131:1, 2, 3 • 1 Thes 2:7b–9, 13 • Mt 23:1–12

Nor are you to be called instructors, for you have one instructor, the Messiah. The greatest among you will be your servant. All who exalt themselves will be humbled, and all who humble themselves will be exalted.

CYCLE B

Second Sunday in Ordinary Time

1 Sam 3:3b–10, 19 • Ps 40:2, 4, 7–8, 8–9, 10 (8a, 9a) • 1 Cor 6:13c–15a, 17–20 • Jn 1:35–42

When Jesus turned and saw them following, he said to them, "What are you looking for?" They said to him, "Rabbi" (which translated means Teacher), "where are you staying?" He said to them, "Come and see."

Third Sunday in Ordinary Time

Jn 3:1–5, 10 • Ps 25:4–5, 6–7, 8–9 (4a) • 1 Cor 7:29–31 • Mk 1:14–20

And Jesus said to them, "Follow me and I will make you fish for people." And immediately they left their nets and followed him.

Second Sunday of Easter

Acts 4:32–35 • Ps 118:2–4, 13–15, 22–24 • 1 Jn 5:1–6 • Jn 20:19–31

Have you believed because you have seen me? Blessed are those who have not seen and yet have come to believe.

Fourth Sunday of Easter

Acts 4:8–12 • Ps 118:1, 8–9, 21–23, 26, 28, 29 (22) • 1 Jn 3:1–2 • Jn 10:11–18

I know my own and my own know me, just as the Father knows me and I know the Father. And I lay down my life for the sheep.

Fifth Sunday of Easter

Acts 9:26–31 • Ps 22:26–27, 28, 30, 31–32 (26a) • 1 Jn 3:18–24 • Jn 15:1–8

I am the vine, you are the branches. Those who abide in me and I in them bear much fruit, because apart from me you can do nothing.

The Holy Trinity

Dt 4:32–34, 39–40 • Ps 33:4–5, 6, 9, 18–19, 20, 22 (12b) • Rom 8:14–17 • Mt 28:16–20

Go therefore and make disciples of all nations, baptizing them in the name of the Father and of the Son and of the Holy Spirit, and teaching them to obey everything that I have commanded you.

Eighteenth Sunday in Ordinary Time

Ex 16:2–4, 12–15 • Ps 78:3–4, 23–24, 25, 54 (24b) • Eph 4:17, 20–24 • Jn 6:24–35

Jesus said to them, "I am the bread of life. Whoever comes to me will never be hungry, and whoever believes in me will never be thirsty."

Twenty-Fourth Sunday in Ordinary Time

Is 50:4–9a • Ps 116:1–2, 3–4, 5–6, 8–9 (9) • Jas 2:14–18 • Mk 8:27–35

He called the crowd with his disciples, and said to them, "If any want to become my followers, let them deny themselves and take up their cross and follow me."

CYCLE C

Baptism of the Lord

Is 42:1–4, 6–7 • Ps 29:1–2, 3–4, 3b, 9b–10 • Acts 10:34–38 • Lk 3:15–16, 21–22

Now when all the people were baptized, and when Jesus also had been baptized and was praying, the heaven was opened, and the Holy Spirit descended upon him.

Second Sunday in Ordinary Time

Is 62:1–5 • Ps 96:1–2, 2–3, 7–8, 9–10 (3) • 1 Cor 12:4–11 • Jn 2:1–11

Jesus did this, the first of his signs, in Cana of Galilee, and revealed his glory; and his disciples believed in him.

Third Sunday in Ordinary Time

Neh 8:2–4a, 5–6, 8–10 • Ps 19:8, 9, 10, 15 • 1 Cor 12:12–30 • Lk 1:1–4; 4:14–21

The Spirit of the Lord is upon me, because he has anointed me to bring good news to the poor.

Fifth Sunday in Ordinary Time

Is 6:1–2a, 3–8 • Ps 138:1–2, 2–3, 4–5, 7–8 (1c) • 1 Cor 15:1–11 • Lk 5:1–11

When they had brought their boats to shore, they left everything and followed him.

Fourth Sunday of Easter

Acts 13:14, 43–52 • Ps 100:1–2, 3, 5 • Rev 7:9, 14b–17 • Jn 10:27–30

I give them eternal life, and they will never perish.

Fifth Sunday of Easter

Acts 14:21–27 • Ps 145:8–9, 10–11, 12–13 • Rev 21:1–5a • Jn 13:31–33a, 34–35

I give you a new commandment, that you love one another. Just as I have loved you, you also should love one another.

Twelfth Sunday in Ordinary Time

Zec 12:10–11 • Ps 63:2, 3–4, 5–6, 8–9 • Gal 3:26–29 • Lk 9:18–24

If any want to become my followers, let them deny themselves and take up their cross daily and follow me.

Thirteenth Sunday in Ordinary Time

1 Kgs 19:16b, 19–21 • Ps 16:1–2, 5, 7–8, 9–10, 11 • Gal 5:1, 13–18 • Lk 9:51–62

To another he said, "Follow me." But he said, "Lord, first let me go and bury my father." But Jesus said to him, "Let the dead bury their own dead; but as for you, go and proclaim the kingdom of God."

Seventeenth Sunday in Ordinary Time
Gn 18:20–32 • Ps 138:1–2, 2–3, 6–7, 7–8 (3a) • Col 2:12–14 • Lk 11:1–13
For everyone who asks receives, and everyone who searches finds, and for everyone who knocks, the door will be opened.

Twentieth Sunday in Ordinary Time
Jer 38:4–6, 8–10 • Ps 40:2, 3, 4, 18 (14b) • Heb 12:1–4 • Lk 12:49–53
I have a baptism with which to be baptized, and what stress I am under until it is completed!

Twenty-Fourth Sunday in Ordinary Time
Ex 32:7–11, 13–14 • Ps 51:3–4, 12–13, 17, 19 • 1 Tm 1:12–17 • Lk 15:1–32
"For this son of mine was dead and is alive again; he was lost and is found!" And they began to celebrate.

Thirtieth Sunday in Ordinary Time
Sir 35:12–14, 16–18 • Ps 34:2–3, 17–18, 19, 23 (7a) • 2 Tm 4:6–8, 16–18 • Lk 18:9–14
All who exalt themselves will be humbled, but all who humble themselves will be exalted.

Christ the King
2 Sm 5:1–3 • Ps 122:1–2, 3–4, 4–5 • Col 1:12–20 • Lk 23:35–43
Then he said, "Jesus, remember me when you come into your kingdom." He replied, "Truly I tell you, today you will be with me in Paradise."

Adaptations

So what is an adaptation, and how do you know when you can make one? Or, another way the question gets asked is, what are the rules we *must* follow? Here are some general principles that might help.

KNOWING THE RULES

The first thing to realize is that "the rules" are not all written down in one place. They appear in a variety of documents that have varying levels of authority. A lower document can't override a higher document. So if there is a conflict, the higher document rules.

There are two broad categories of documents: universal and United States. (Or Canada, or Mexico, or whatever country or region you are in.)

Under universal documents, the most authoritative, there are three types:

1. *Conciliar constitutions*; examples include:
   - The Constitution on the Sacred Liturgy
   - The Constitution on the Church

2. *Liturgical laws* for select rites; examples include:
   - The General Instruction of the Roman Missal
   - Introduction, Lectionary for Mass
   - General Norms for the Liturgical Year and the Calendar

3. *Directories*; for example:
   - Directory for Masses with Children

For the United States church, there are two kinds of documents:

1. *Norms* approved by the U.S. bishops; examples include:
   - Norms for the Distribution and Reception of Holy Communion in the Diocese of the United States
   - The National Statutes for the Catechumenate

2. *Documents* issued by the U.S. bishops; examples include:
   - Music in Catholic Worship
   - Built of Living Stones: Art, Architecture, and Worship
   - Fulfilled in Your Hearing: The Homily in the Sunday Assembly

So when you are struggling with adaptations, always keep the primary teaching in mind. The prime directive for all liturgy is the full, conscious, and active participation of the assembly (see Constitution on the Sacred Liturgy, 14). Any adaptation you make that reduces assembly participation is not an adaptation you want to make.

READ THE INTRODUCTIONS

Next look at the ritual itself. Every rite, including the RCIA, has a pastoral introduction that explains the purpose of the rite. (These introductions, along with the rubrics or instructions in the rite itself, are in the category of liturgical laws above, which are equal in weight to canon law.) Usually the purpose of the rite is stated in the very first paragraph. Look at RCIA, 1. Without reading anything else, we know the RCIA is

- for adults
- who seek the living God
- and want to live by faith.

With God's help, the rites will

- strengthen them spiritually
- and will prepare them to celebrate the sacraments fruitfully

Any adaptations you make must keep that primary goal always at the forefront.

An "adaptation" that parishes often make is to initiate the catechumens before they have celebrated one full liturgical year with the community. However, this adaptation violates the primary goal of the RCIA—to strengthen the candidates spiritually and prepare them to celebrate the sacraments fruitfully.

Keep reading through the introduction (in the RCIA or any rite), and you will find specific instances where the rite tells you to adapt. In the RCIA, for example, see 2, 3, 8, 16, 17, 19, 23, 24, and 26-30.

And even if you don't go looking at all those right now, you have to get out your big yellow highlighter and read paragraph 35. Make sure you highlight this sentence:

> …ministers, according to their prudent pastoral judgment, may accommodate the rite to the circumstances of the candidates and others who are present.

START SEEING RED

Another key to adaptation is to read the small print within the ritual text itself. These instructions are called *rubrics* (from the Latin, *rubrīca*, which my dictionary says means "red chalk"). In some study editions, these sections actually are in red.

If you turn to the Rite of Acceptance (48), you'll see the entire first page is almost all rubrics. Under the Opening Dialogue, just before the priest's first scripted text, the rubrics say, "One of the following *or something similar* may be used" (emphasis added).

If you link that with what you just highlighted in paragraph 35, the obvious conclusion is you are going to adapt! What possible reason could there be for using a canned script when the rite is clearly urging you to create something that will fit your catechumens and your parish?

 Sometimes a rubric will list two or three options. The preferred option (in the eyes of those who designed the rite) is always listed first. As a general rule, the first option best meets the primary goal of the rite as a whole.

KNOW YOUR AUDIENCE

That leads to the next level of adaptation. You have to adapt for the culture in which you find yourself. This isn't necessarily just a difference between, say, Hispanic and Anglo cultures. I once worked in a parish that was pretty homogenous. The majority of parishioners were from the same ethnic background, same income bracket, same political leanings. But there were two different worship spaces, upstairs (more formal) and downstairs (more informal). Sometimes all-parish meetings felt as fractured as the Mideast peace negotiations. Obviously the adaptations you might make for the upstairs liturgies would be different than for the downstairs community.

OUR BEST SELVES

The final level of adaptation is one that I don't hear talked about much. Good liturgy planners are not ritual car dealers. The liturgy cannot be ordered in the size and color anyone wants. Our adaptations have to be a little bit challenging, urging us to take up the Cross and giving us the strength to do so. Sometimes the adaptation is not what a community wants but what it needs. A good example of this is the first rubric for the Rite of Acceptance: "The candidates, their sponsors, and a group of the faithful gather outside the church (or inside at the entrance or elsewhere) or at some other site suitable for this rite" (48).

The first choice, gathering outside, is the preferred choice. Many parishes, however, choose the "elsewhere" option, gathering comfortably inside the church as we do every Sunday. In some communities, like the upstairs worshippers in my former parish, this can be very sensible. Too much change all at once is not going to help them fully participate. However, I know of parishes that have been making that pastoral accommodation for a decade or more. At some point, it is not pastoral to compromise for people's comfort zones simply so as not to rock the boat.

 When choosing adaptations, always ask, what is the ideal option? And if we cannot meet the ideal this time, what steps will we take to move closer to the ideal next time?

Annulments

Dealing with annulment issues can be difficult. Many Catholics often do not understand everything the church teaches about marriage (and divorce), and inquirers certainly don't. Many of those seeking initiation or reception into full communion do not even think about raising previous marriages as something to be discussed. So let's look at a few of the basic things a catechumenate team needs to know about marriage and annulments.

WHAT IS MARRIAGE?

The *Catechism of the Catholic Church* can be helpful here. Get a copy (or access it online) and read through paragraphs 1621-1642. Note a few important things about marriage. First, it is the *consent* of the couples (the "I do") that "makes the marriage" (1626).

Another important thing is the *way* the consent is given (or the *form*). For Catholics, that consent needs to take place in front of an ordained priest or deacon, but for non-Catholics, it does not. If two Lutherans say "I do" in a way that is proper for Lutherans, their marriage is a valid marriage. If two Jews get married in a Jewish service, that is a valid marriage. If two unbaptized people skydive out of a Cessna over Vegas with an Elvis-impersonating-minister and exchange vows before popping their chutes, that is a valid marriage. So consent is necessary, and proper form is necessary (1631).

If a couple gives valid consent to each other, and if they do so in the correct form, they are bonded together forever by God's love and their love for each other (1639-1651).

WHAT ABOUT MARRIAGES THAT FAIL?

Being human, we cannot always live up to the ideal marriage that God and the church (and we ourselves!) would want for us. In some cases, remaining together becomes impossible. In that case, spouses can separate and even get a civil divorce. But a couple that was validly married, even though now civilly divorced, cannot remarry and still participate in the sacraments of the church (1648-1650).

WHAT IS AN ANNULMENT?

An annulment is not a divorce. A valid marriage can never be dissolved. But how do we know if the marriage was valid? There are a number of things that might have caused the consent or the form to be lacking. You don't necessarily need to know what all those things are, but you do need to know the difference between a divorce and an annulment. A divorce is a dissolution of a marriage. In the eyes of the church, if two people are validly married, that marriage cannot be dissolved. We believe this because we understand married love to be an extension of and a symbol of God's divine love. Just as we can never be "divorced" from God's love, we can never divorce from authentic, valid marital love (1639-1640).

But, in some cases, the marriage was not authentic. It may not have met the requirements for validity and can therefore be declared "null." An annulment is a declaration by the church that a valid marriage never took place. Something was wrong with the consent or the form that, if it had been evident at the time, would have prevented the marriage from happening in the first place (1629).

WHAT TO DO WITH DIVORCED INQUIRERS

It is important to discover the inquirer's marital status early in the process. For inquirers who were previously married and are remarried or intend to remarry, you should assume they will need an annulment before they can be initiated or received into full communion. There are possible exceptions.

For example, unbaptized inquirers may not need an annulment. Or a baptized inquirer who was married with an incorrect form may not need an annulment. But you usually won't be the one making that call. It's easiest to start with the assumption that an annulment will be needed.

 You will also need to discover the marital status of the inquirer's spouse or fiancée. If the spouse of an inquirer is divorced and remarried, he or she will need to get an annulment before the inquirer can celebrate the sacraments of the church.

However! You do not want to lead with the rules. You don't want to start by saying something to the effect of: Here's what you did wrong, and here's what you need to do to fix it before we can go on. As with everything in the inquiry stage, you want to start by listening.

Ask sincere and open-ended questions about the inquirer's past relationships. What about those relationships has led him to this point in his life? How did he meet his current spouse or fiancée? How has that relationship strengthened him? Listen closely. Listen for the movement of the Spirit in the inquirer's life. Help the inquirer recognize how God has been present in everything that has happened.

As you are having this conversation (or conversations), talk about your own marriage. (If you are single, talk about your parents' marriage or a friend's marriage.) Discuss how the church sees your marriage as a vocation and as a participation in the divine love of God. Discuss how you try to make your marriage a visible witness to the love of Christ in the world.

Remember, your goal in the inquiry stage is not to teach all the rules in the *Catechism*. It is to move the inquirer to conversion to Christ. If we really believe what we say about marriage, we need to talk about our own marriages (or those of our loved ones) in such a way that it is clear to the inquirers just what is at stake. It needs to become clear that we don't believe in divorce not just because the church says so but because we are truly caught up in God's never-ending love through our marriages.

Those who are not familiar with the annulment process sometimes assume a declaration of nullity means the marriage never existed at all. While the *Catechism* does use that language (1629), it is speaking of a sacramental (or potentially sacramental) marriage that is a vocational ministry of Christ. By declaring the marriage null, the church is saying that kind of marriage did not exist. According to civil law, and probably in the hearts of the ex-spouses, the marriage did exist. The church isn't denying that. Another worry folks sometimes have is that getting an annulment means their children will be "illegitimate." That is not the case. The legal or moral status of a couple's children remains exactly the same after an annulment is granted.

BRINGING UP ANNULMENT

If the previously married inquirer is coming to a point of conversion, and it is becoming clearer that he will want to move on to the next step in the initiation process, you will need to encourage him to seek an annulment. If you have been

THE ANNULMENT PROCESS

The divorced person asks to be heard by the church. (This is a formal, written request that a parish minister will assist with.)

The parish minister sends all the necessary information to a diocesan office called the tribunal.

The tribunal considers the person's request and, in the end, returns an answer stating that the first marriage is considered either valid or null by the church.

As part of the process, the tribunal will contact the former spouse if possible. The former spouse has a right to participate in the process if he or she wishes. Some cases also require information from witnesses to the marriage. The annulment minister can explain more about the details of this.

The time for the entire process varies from case to case, but it is usually about one year. (It could take longer.)

There is a fee for the process that covers administrative costs and salaries. The fee varies from diocese to diocese. (The average cost is $500; check with your tribunal.) However, no one is ever denied access to the annulment process because they cannot afford the fee.

discussing the church's teaching on marriage and your own marriage, it should be pretty clear to the inquirer why an annulment is necessary. If it is not clear, that may be a sign he isn't ready yet to move out of the inquiry stage. Obviously, if *you* have been through an annulment, it will be easier to discuss the subject with the inquirer. If that's not the case for you, perhaps someone else on your team has been through one. Or perhaps there is a parishioner, possibly a potential sponsor, who might join you for the discussion.

In any case, when it is time to raise the issue, *keep listening.* Divorce is one of the most painful human experiences. No matter how long ago it was and no matter how happy a person is in his or her current relationship, he or she is likely to still feel pain and regret and possibly guilt about the divorce. Listen to the hurt, and try to empathize as best you can. Try to avoid pat statements such as, "An annulment is a healing experience," or "It isn't as bad as it sounds." If that was true for you in your own annulment process, sure, speak about your experience. But don't assume that the inquirer's experience will be the same.

When discussing the annulment process, keep your description general. (See the sidebar for a simple outline of the process.) Find out who on your parish staff (often it is the pastor) deals with annulments, and let that person go into all the details. If you think the inquirer might not have to go through the annulment process for some reason, don't offer that promise. Let the pastor or other annulment minister discuss the possible exceptions for particular cases.

THE RULES

There is nothing in the RCIA about remarried people entering the process. The Rite assumes that everyone entering the process is free to do so, without impediment. So that means you need to make sure there are no impediments before an inquirer starts the process. In most dioceses (check with yours), inquirers who have a marriage impediment may celebrate the Rite of Acceptance (or Call to Continuing Conversion) as long as they have begun the annulment process. However, it is your responsibility to make it *excruciatingly clear* that they cannot celebrate the Rite of Election (and therefore cannot be initiated) until the annulment is granted. And they need to be aware that the annulment might not be granted. If the church finds the first marriage *was* valid, and the inquirer is remarried, he or she may not celebrate the sacraments.

If the inquirer has not remarried and does not intend to remarry, he or she has no impediment. The impediment is not the civil divorce itself, because the church does not recognize that. It is the second marriage that prevents an inquirer from celebrating the sacraments. So someone who is merely divorced and doesn't intend to remarry can be initiated or received into the church. However, it is your responsibility to make it *excruciatingly clear* that if they ever do decide to remarry, they will first need to obtain an annulment before they can do so.